On the Road to

Roxton, Texas

More Wisdom from a Small Town Pastor

I0157746

Louis A. Holmes

MaxHolt
Media

Cover design by Louis A. Holmes & Eddie Holt
Cover art Louis A. Holmes
ISBN: 978-1-944537-16-6

Published by: Max Holt Media
303 Cascabel Place,
Mount Juliet, TN 37122
www.maxholtmedia.com
On facebook at www.facebook.com/maxholtmedia
   Email – max@maxholtmedia.com
   Twitter - @maxholtmedia

Additional books by Louis Holmes:
WHERE IN THE WORLD IS ROXTON, TEXAS?
   Available in both paperback and Kindle editions.

INTRODUCTION

I'm a bi-vocational pastor of a small church in a small town. I have a full-time job with an electric utility, but my love is at that small church in that small town. Every morning I get up and drive to work along remote highways and farm roads in route to the utility. Along the way I will see cows pasturing on the rolling hills. The cows are usually grazing on the lush grasses in the mornings and sitting on the ground in the evening chewing their cuds. The digestive system of a cow is remarkable the way that they can eat their grasses without fully chewing, and then burp up balls of grass to chew fully a little later.

It's one thing to go to work in the morning; it's another to be on my way home, on the road back to Roxton, Texas. They say that where you hang your hat is home, and I hang my hat in Roxton.

When I first went to Roxton as pastor of First Baptist Church, I was asked to write articles for the newspaper, the **Roxton Progress**. It is published twice a month, so there isn't too much pressure to meet deadlines. The editor of the paper suggested that I compile my articles and publish them in a book. Because of space constraints in the paper, most of my articles are around 600 words. I feel additional liberty to write in a book format, so some chapters are a bit longer; some are shorter. The purpose of my articles in the paper is simply encouragement. I will write about something humorous or thought-provoking from my youth and then make an inspirational application. As of the date of this writing, these articles have not been published in the paper but the LORD willing, one day most of them will.

After you read a chapter, read the verses following that chapter. Then go for a few days, thinking about what you read. Take the time to *chew the cud.* I pray that it will make a difference in your life in some small way.

DEDICATION

To my grandchildren:

Jovie and Zed

May the Lord God richly bless you.

NOTE: This book is arranged by **Chapter Number** rather than **page number**. Search for individual subjects based on their **Chapter Numbers**.

CONTENTS

1

Chewin' the Cud

I am a bi-vocational pastor in a small town called Roxton, Texas. I'm employed with an electric utility company a few miles away, earning a salary with insurance and retirement benefits. The church is small, so the free time I have is adequate to meet the needs of the people.

My drive to work takes me through some towns that are smaller than Roxton. On each side of the highway I see lots of cows pasturing in the rolling hills. Calves stay close to their mothers; usually one or two calves are nursing. Now that spring has come, the cows are out there eating grass in the morning and chewing their cuds in the afternoon.

I've read that cows have four stomachs. God, in his marvelous wisdom created the cattle for the life which they live. God created the cattle on the sixth day of creation, along with other beasts for the benefit of man. All life was given the herbs of the ground to eat, even the dinosaurs. Cows have been eating grassy type foods for a long time.

A cow has four stomachs, each one fulfilling its part of the digestion process. Technically, a cow has one stomach with four compartments. The first compartment is the Rumen, which is the first part of the cow's stomach. It helps break down complex plant products like grass. The second compartment is the Reticulum. Here the food mixes with the cow's saliva and produces cud. Cows burp up the cud into their mouths and chew it to help break the grass fibers down further. When you see a cow that looks like she is chomping on bubble gum, really she is chewing her cud. The third compartment is the Omasum; here all the water is absorbed out of the food. Finally, there is the Abomasum where the food is finally digested, similar to what happens in a human stomach.

For the cow, it is actually a very efficient system. She can graze all day and not have to chew the food completely, but just enough to send it to the first compartment. Later, when she has time, she can chew her cud to further the digestion process. In the summertime she will lay under a shade tree and chew her cud. You might say that she is giving further thought to digesting her food.

Christian people will hear a great lesson or sermon but unless further thought is given to what they have heard, it might be forgotten, or undigested as it were, thus making it impossible to absorb all the good things they heard from the Word of God. The Word of God is rich with truth and application. Further thought is necessary to complete the application to our lives.

The idea of chewing the cud is simply an illustration of how we need to spend time rehearsing what we have heard. It does not bother a cow that she will burp up something previously eaten to digest it further by chewing. Likewise, Christian people should carve time out of their day for further study in the Word of God and in prayer.

"Whom shall he teach knowledge? and
whom shall he make to understand

doctrine? them that are weaned from the
milk, and drawn from the breasts. For
precept must be upon precept, precept upon
precept; line upon line, line upon line; here a
little, and there a little:"
Isaiah 28:9-10

One of the thoughts here is that we must grow. The Bible is full of simple things that many people hold to tightly, but they are still feeding on milk, and need to be weaned. The apostle Paul spoke of this as well.

"For every one that useth milk is unskilful in
the word of righteousness: for he is a babe.
But strong meat belongeth to them that are
of full age, even those who by reason of use
have their senses exercised to discern both
good and evil."
Hebrews 5:13-14

If you had a baby who never developed as it should, a trip to the doctor would be in order. At a certain age it should learn to turn over, crawl, and eventually walk. Similarly, Pastors see so many people in church who have never grown in the Lord. We pray for them and love them, desiring they would become inquisitive and seek more from the Word of God. Unfortunately, they never chew the cud.

Perhaps people are simply too busy, and the world provides numerous distractions that usually have little value for our lives. If people are consistently yielding to the distractions, they will never have the time to digest the Word.

When we get into the meat of the Word of God, sometimes we will not comprehend what is in the scriptures. Further thought and study is necessary to keep us strong. Christians who believe only what little they read and study in the church service is sufficient, are woefully mistaken.

"Study to shew thyself approved unto God,
a workman that needeth not to be
ashamed, rightly dividing the word of
truth."
II Timothy 2:15

As my teachers often said in school, "There will be a test." And in the Christian life there will be a test. Abraham was tested when God commanded that he offer his son Isaac as a sacrifice. I believe that Abraham knew that God controlled all things, and that God would provide, which He did.

We can learn much from the cows, one of God's great creations. Also, we can learn great principles from the way in which they digest food. So when you hear the Word, find yourself a quiet spot with no distractions of the world, and "chew the cud" a while to further digest what God has for you.

ADDITIONAL SCRIPTURES:

"This book of the law shall not depart out of thy mouth; but thou shalt meditate therein day and night, that thou mayest observe to do according to all that is written therein: for then thou shalt make thy way prosperous, and then thou shalt have good success."
Joshua 1:8

"Let the words of my mouth, and the meditation of my heart, be acceptable in thy sight, O LORD, my strength, and my redeemer."
Psalm 19:14

"I will meditate in thy precepts, and have respect unto thy ways."
Psalm 119:15

"My meditation of him shall be sweet: I will be glad in the LORD."
Psalm 104:34

"My mouth shall speak of wisdom; and the meditation of my heart shall be of understanding."
Psalm 49:3

"But thou, when thou prayest, enter into thy

closet, and when thou hast shut thy door,
pray to thy Father which is in secret; and thy
Father which seeth in secret shall reward
thee openly."
Matthew 6:6

Notes:

2

Thoughts about the Round Bale

Driving around the Roxton area you can see the round bales of hay everywhere. A time or two I have watched the machine that makes the round bale as it's pulled behind a tractor. When finished, the bales are scattered over the field ready for transport and placing into storage. I think it's a beautiful sight to see the bales all in a row at the edge of the field. Since I'm a city boy I've never had the privilege of baling hay; square or round. I have heard that square bales are a lot more work so perhaps the lowly round bale has its merits.

It's fascinating that farmers and ranchers can harvest the hay in summer and store it in the round bale for use in the winter. It is truly an ingenious way of harvesting food for the animals. I am sure that the cows are thankful for it during the winter. The round bale represents goodness of the summer preserved for winter.

The Bible says in Psalm 33:5,

> *"The earth is full of the goodness of the LORD."*

The inhabitants of the earth complain so much that they have become blinded to the goodness of God. The sun rises every day on the evil and the good. The rain falls on the just and the unjust alike. Truly the hand of God is full of mercy in all of His creation.

The Word of God also says that the rain falls in the wilderness where no man is!

"Who hath divided a watercourse for the overflowing of waters, or a way for the lightning of thunder; To cause it to rain on the earth, where no man is; on the wilderness, wherein there is no man; To satisfy the desolate and waste ground; and to cause the bud of the tender herb to spring forth?"
Job 38:25-27

Christians need a harvest now of the Word of God which can be used later when needed. It is important that we read and memorize Scripture. Anyone can do it, young and old alike.

I have heard some of the senior citizens tell me it is too hard to memorize Scripture, but they can sure tell me the names of their twelve great-grandchildren! Birthdays too!

Memorizing Scripture is a rewarding experience. Your mind becomes saturated with the Word of God, which is in itself a source of power for the believer. Your thoughts and attitudes are more in tune with our Heavenly Father. The fullness of His love permeates your being.

So who knows, perhaps the next time you see a round bale of hay you will remember that the earth is full of the goodness of the LORD. And that would be a good time to practice what you have learned.

ADDITIONAL SCRIPTURES:

"He that gathereth in summer is a wise son: but he that sleepeth in harvest is a son that causeth shame."
Proverbs 10:5

"While the earth remaineth, seedtime and harvest, and cold and heat, and summer and winter, and day and night shall not cease."
Genesis 8:22

"Honour the LORD with thy substance, and with the firstfruits of all thine increase:"
Proverbs 3:9

"And let us not be weary in well doing: for in due season we shall reap, if we faint not."
Galatians 6:9

"Now the parable is this: The seed is the word of God."
Luke 8:11

"Truth shall spring out of the earth; and righteousness shall look down from heaven. Yea, the Lord shall give that which is good; and our land shall yield her increase."
Psalm 85:11-12

Notes

3

Going into a Briar Patch

The subject of tithes and offerings can be tough for the preacher like a child taking a short cut across a briar patch (To us folks back home it was sticker burrs!). God's financial plan for His Church is the members will practice obedience and love in their giving. When the members fail to give, it can cause financial hardships and embarrassment for the church and its vendors.

I have seen churches where the finances are terribly managed. In my humble opinion, the finances of the church should be in the capable hands of the treasurer and monitored by the pastor and the congregation. I do not believe a pastor should act as the treasurer or assistant treasurer unless it is absolutely necessary.

As for giving, the principle of tithing is taught in the Old Testament. Abraham tithed. As did others in the Old Testament.

Jesus Christ Himself mentioned tithing and the hypocritical way that the Pharisees went about it. He mentioned tithing a couple of times of those holding to the Old Testament, like the Pharisees, who would tithe on the least little portion and yet did not exercise any love.

"But woe unto you, Pharisees! for ye tithe
mint and rue and all manner of herbs, and
pass over judgment and the love of God:
these ought ye to have done, and not

to leave the other undone."
Luke 11:42

What is taught about giving in the New Testament might surprise you. We are taught to give very generously, and not to be limited to a 10 percent tithe. Let's look at the offerings of the widow.

"And he looked up, and saw the rich men casting their gifts into the treasury. And he saw also a certain poor widow casting in thither two mites. And he said, Of a truth I say unto you, that this poor widow hath cast in more than they all: For all these have of their abundance cast in unto the offerings of God: but she of her penury hath cast in all the living that she had."
Luke 21:1-4

The word *"penury"* can be rendered *deep poverty*. So this widow lady, who would have had a very tough time in Jesus day, cast in just two mites, but it was all she had. Let's apply that to today. Let say that you went to the bank, and drew out your 401k retirement, all your savings, and wipe out your bank account, the inheritance for your kids, and you gave that as an offering to the Lord. Then and only then would you be as the widow that gave all she had.

I am not advocating we do just that, unless you feel led of the LORD God to do so. My point is this, for the most part we hold to the teaching of tithing ten percent as taught in the Old Testament, and I believe God is pleased with our obedience. When it comes to offerings, we think of passing the plate in church. Folks will dig around in their pockets and find a couple of dollars to pitch them into the plate.

What about a *real* offering; something given to the LORD which is very precious? The lambs offered on the altar in the Old Testament were the best they had.

> *"Ye shall offer at your own will a male*
> *without blemish, of the beeves, of the*
> *sheep, or of the goats. But whatsoever hath*
> *a blemish, that shall ye not offer: for it shall*
> *not be acceptable for you."*
> *Leviticus 22:19-20*

For example, perhaps you come out on the sweet end of a business deal; why not give an offering of what was more than you expected? If, in the deal you are to make 100 dollars and you make 125 dollars, why not give the extra 25 dollars unto the LORD? You were not expecting it anyway, and God has just given you an opportunity to honor Him. If you give the unexpected amount, you are showing that you love the LORD more than the money. But the truth is, we generally get real stingy when it comes to money. Remember the widow who gave all she had?

When we give an offering over and above the tithe we are saying that the LORD God means more to us than a financial gain, and we trust Him to take care of us. It is at this point we begin to honor the LORD God and take

Him at His word.

I like what the prophet Malachi recorded regarding trusting in the LORD. God said *"Prove me now!"* Isn't it about time we begin to prove the LORD; that we indeed trust Him to take care of us?

God did not promise you would be wealthy. He did not promise you material possessions. But He did promise life eternal for all those who believe on Him.

I have heard it said that you cannot out-give God. I believe that to be true. Further, God owns everything anyway.

> *"The earth is the LORD's, and the fullness thereof; the world, and they that dwell therein."*
> *Psalm 24:1*

God owns you and your wealth. It is God who gives you a life and the ability to earn wealth. God is simply allowing you to be a steward of what He has given you. It is God who allows us to purchase a house or a new car. It is He who allows you all the comforts of this life with the wealth He has given you.

Giving the tithe is obedience unto God. The offering is above and beyond the tithe, and is a pure form of worship, for when we give back to the LORD, we are acknowledging that we need Him more than we need the money. Our giving generously unto the LORD allows Him to meet all our needs in the most unexpected ways.

ADDITIONAL SCRIPTURES:

"Every man shall give as he is able, according to the blessing of the LORD thy God which he hath given thee."
Deuteronomy 16:17

"He coveteth greedily all the day long: but the righteous giveth and spareth not."
Proverbs 21:26

"But this I say, He which soweth sparingly shall reap also sparingly; and he which soweth bountifully shall reap also bountifully."
II Corinthians 9:6

"Give, and it shall be given unto you; good measure, pressed down, and shaken together, and running over, shall men give into your bosom. For with the same measure that ye mete withal it shall be measured to you again."
Luke 6:38

"The liberal soul shall be made fat: and he that watereth shall be watered also himself."
Proverbs 11:25

"Honour the Lord with thy substance, and

*with the firstfruits of all thine increase: So
shall thy barns be filled with plenty, and thy
presses shall burst out with new wine.
Proverbs 3:9-10*

Notes:

4

Thoughts about Climate Change

In the early 1960's, living in the parsonage behind the church, I would spend most of my time outside playing. In the summertime the sun would beat down and everything became hot. The gravel in the parking lot, toys left in the sun, everything became almost too hot to touch. Mom knew the importance of keeping me hydrated so she did something special just for me.

When Mom would buy laundry supplies, she would buy bleach in the quart bottles. When she used all the bleach in the bottle, she would rinse it out, remove the label, and fill the bottle with water. The bleach bottle went into the refrigerator so I would have cool water to drink anytime I wanted. When I was outside I thought about the bottle of water a lot. The heat was unbelievable. I would quit what I was doing to go get a refreshing drink of cool and clean water.

The bleach bottle was perfect for that. It was the original bottled water. Most cities will treat the water system with a little bleach to kill microbes and make the water safe to drink. The bottle was rinsed out before use so there was no danger to me.

I also remember when a cold front would come in the springtime bringing thunderstorms that were fierce. The winters also were cold with periodic snow. No one said anything about global warming back then.

The world is all abuzz about climate change. So is there a warming of the planet? What does God say?

Science forms its theories by observation. I have no doubt that there are observable changes in the temperature and weather patterns of the earth; more rain, hotter temperatures, fiercer storms. All is a part of our earth.

God is in full control of our weather. In the New Testament, Jesus had sent His disciples to another place which was across a body of water. In the night a storm arose, and the disciples, who were seasoned fishermen, became afraid. Jesus was asleep in the boat. The disciples woke Him, asking Jesus to save them. Since the disciples were masters at boating and fishing, they had obviously been in storms before. This time, they were afraid.

> *"And, behold, there arose a great tempest in the sea, insomuch that the ship was covered with the waves: but he was asleep. And his disciples came to him, and awoke him, saying, Lord, save us: we perish. And he saith unto them, Why are ye fearful, O ye of little faith? Then he arose, and rebuked the winds and the sea; and there was a great calm. But the men marvelled, saying, What manner of man is this, that even the winds and the sea obey him!"*
> *Matthew 8:24-27*

Knowing how Jesus is the Creator of all things, He would have no problem in calming the storm. He is in control.

One of the catch-phrases is "man-made" climate

change. God has established the laws of physics; they are steady as He created them. The speed of light, the speed of sound, the ways certain materials interact with each other, all are ordained of God. I believe it is possible that pollution from cars and planes can have an influence on our atmosphere. God gave man dominion over the earth in Genesis Chapter One. So if we build and run enough cars, we can create a haze over the city.

I remember pictures of the Los Angeles skyline years ago and the haze in the air. To clean up the air we have improved the technology of refining gasoline and oil, and we have also improved our automobiles to pollute less. An example of that is when I was a kid, we had to change our oil every 2,000 miles and tune the car with new spark plugs every 10,000 miles. Now it is much different. My new car gets an oil change every ten thousand miles and tune up every one hundred thousand miles.

Even with such improvements in automobiles, the problem is the number of cars on the road. It will take a while for other technologies to be developed to reduce our pollution.

However, I do not worry about climate change. Did it ever occur to you that nothing occurs to God? God knew from the halls of eternity that someday man would be dealing with what we call *climate change*. I do not deny that a change may exist, but we need to be good citizens of the earth and keep our focus on worshiping the Creator. It is a mistake for us to worship creation. The earth and the skies are certainly beautiful, but we worship the LORD God who created them all.

ADDITIONAL SCRIPTURES:

"But our God is in the heavens: he hath done whatsoever he hath pleased."
Psalm 115:3

"And he arose, and rebuked the wind, and said unto the sea, Peace, be still. And the wind ceased, and there was a great calm. And he said unto them, Why are ye so fearful? how is it that ye have no faith? And they feared exceedingly, and said one to another, What manner of man is this, that even the wind and the sea obey him?"
Mark 4:39-41

"He stretcheth out the north over the empty place, and hangeth the earth upon nothing."
Job 26:7

"Who hath divided a watercourse for the overflowing of waters, or a way for the lightning of thunder; To cause it to rain on the earth, where no man is; on the wilderness, wherein there is no man; To satisfy the desolate and waste ground; and to cause the bud of the tender herb to spring forth?"
Job 38:25-27

"I would seek unto God, and unto God would I commit my cause: Which doeth great things and unsearchable; marvellous things without number: Who giveth rain upon the earth, and sendeth waters upon the fields:"
Job 5:8-10

"Fire, and hail; snow, and vapours; stormy wind fulfilling his word:"
Psalm 148:8

Notes:

5

The Disadvantage of a Dull Axe

The electric utility deals with a lot of wooden poles to build our power lines. Most of our poles are Southern Yellow Pine that are treated with a preservative to prevent rot and damage by insects. A lot of our new wood poles are used to replace older poles installed years ago.

At times a pole will be sit in the ground where water does not drain properly, and the pole will ruin faster. Sometimes a pole is hit by a car or truck. In either case it must be changed out to ensure system reliability.

The lineman will set the new pole next to the old pole and then transfer the wires to the new pole. He will use a chain saw as necessary to remove short pieces of the old pole for clearance. For the lineman, the saw must be sharp, otherwise the process of removing the old pole can become dangerous.

People do not use axes much anymore since the advent of the chain saw. However, when you use an axe, the result is much better when it's sharp. If the axe is dull, the work is much harder.

"If the iron be blunt, and he do not whet the edge, then must he put to more strength: but wisdom is profitable to direct."
Ecclesiastes 10:10

Solomon makes a brilliant analogy here about a dull axe or similar tools. It takes more work and sweat to accomplish the task. Similarly, a mind that is dull of wisdom will have to work harder to accomplish that task of life.

I work with wood and know the importance of a sharp tool. If I am turning a piece of wood on the lathe, it is very important that the cutting tool be sharp. If I cut wood on the table saw, then the blade must be sharp. It will yield better and safer results.

No matter your age, it is important that we learn wisdom to have a sharp mind. Solomon had more to say:

"Then said I, Wisdom is better
than strength:"
Ecclesiastes 9:16

I have seen people who do not exercise wisdom, and their strength is exhausted trying to live this life. You can chop down a tree with a dull axe, but the work will be very hard.

The advantage we are after is to have the wisdom in our lives which comes from the LORD.

"How much better is it to get wisdom than
gold! and to get understanding rather to be
chosen than silver!"
Proverbs 16:16

The choice of wisdom is to your advantage. It is not just any wisdom; it is the wisdom of the LORD. God desires that we live life abundantly. We do that with His wisdom.

Additional Scriptures

"Iron sharpeneth iron; so a man sharpeneth the countenance of his friend."
Proverbs 27:17

"The fear of the LORD is the beginning of wisdom: a good understanding have all they that do his commandments: his praise endureth forever."
Psalm 111:10

"The fear of the LORD is the beginning of wisdom: and the knowledge of the holy is understanding."
Proverbs 9:10

"The fear of the LORD is the beginning of knowledge: but fools despise wisdom and instruction."
Proverbs 1:7

"And unto man he said, Behold, the fear of the LORD, that is wisdom; and to depart from evil is understanding."
Job 28:28

"The proverbs of Solomon the son of David, king of Israel; To know wisdom and instruction; to perceive the words of understanding; To receive the instruction of

wisdom, justice, and judgment, and equity;
To give subtilty to the simple, to the young
man knowledge and discretion. A wise man
will hear, and will increase learning; and a
man of understanding shall attain unto wise
counsels: To understand a proverb, and the
interpretation; the words of the wise, and
their dark sayings."
Proverbs 1:1-6

Notes:

6

Yes, No, and Wait

Have you every prayed to God and impatiently waited for the answer? If so you are not alone.

God is Sovereign; that means He exercises supreme authority in heaven and earth, and in eternity and time. While God is Sovereign He also allows man the dignity of free will, meaning that we can make the choices we desire in our lives. Interestingly, while God desires for us to choose to love and serve Him, He does not force us to so. If God had us all on strings directing our every move, we would not be much more than a planet of marionettes.

God also knows our frailty as humans. The Bible says in Psalm 103:14,

> *"For he knoweth our frame; he*
> *remembereth that we are dust."*

So when we pray to Him He is gracious to answer…Yes, No, and Wait.

God is not only Sovereign, He is also omniscient, meaning that God is all-knowing. When we pray to Him, He always knows what is best for us. We might want God to move right now, but in His righteous omniscience His answer is wait. God, in His infinite mercy, always extends His goodness to us. It might be hard to imagine that waiting is better than yes or no, but God always knows best.

I think when God tells us to wait, He is telling us to be patient.

"Be still, and know that I am God: I will be exalted among the heathen, I will be exalted in the earth."
Psalm 46:10

We forget that God will be lifted up and exalted, and in our impatience we are exercising our will rather than His. Do you remember the joke about the man who prayed "Lord, give me patience, and give it to me right now!"?

"Wait on the LORD: be of good courage, and he shall strengthen thine heart: wait, I say, on the LORD."
Psalm 27:14

I am just as bad as anyone else. I would like to see God move quickly in Roxton, a revival break out, and men and women moved towards the wooing of the Gospel message. God has lessons for both you and me to learn.

"Wait on the Lord, and keep his way, and he shall exalt thee to inherit the land: when the wicked are cut off, thou shalt see it."
Psalm 37:34

The Prophet Elijah confronted an evil King Ahab in I Kings 17. He prophesied that it would not rain. The King and queen of Israel then wanted to kill Elijah. I believe the thing Elijah desired the most was a revival of the people of Israel to abandon idolatry and to return unto the LORD, the Living God. However, Elijah did not see that revival. He saw the miracle of the oil and the meal for the woman of Zarapath; he prayed and fire fell from heaven from the Living God; Elijah even found out that the LORD spoke in a still small voice, not a mighty earthquake or a mighty wind. It was not until his apprentice Elisha came along did Israel have a returning to the LORD.

In all this the LORD was telling Elijah to wait. The work he did prepared the way for a revival of Israel.

Finally, words from the Apostle Paul,

> *"I have planted, Apollos watered;*
> *but God gave the increase."*
> *I Corinthians 3:6*

In God's time He will be exalted. The church in Roxton needs to do nothing else but praise Him to the community. And when it is time, the answer will be "yes."

ADDITIONAL SCRIPTURES:

> *"But they that wait upon the LORD shall*
> *renew their strength; they shall mount up*
> *with wings as eagles; they shall run, and not*
> *be weary; and they shall walk, and not*
> *faint."*
> *Isaiah 40:31*

"The LORD is good unto them that wait for him, to the soul that seeketh him."
Lamentations 3:25

"And it shall be said in that day, Lo, this is our God; we have waited for him, and he will save us: this is the LORD; we have waited for him, we will be glad and rejoice in his salvation."
Isaiah 25:9

"But without faith it is impossible to please him: for he that cometh to God must believe that he is, and that he is a rewarder of them that diligently seek him."
Hebrews 11:6

"And not only so, but we glory in tribulations also: knowing that tribulation worketh patience; And patience, experience; and experience, hope: And hope maketh not ashamed; because the love of God is shed abroad in our hearts by the Holy Ghost which is given unto us."
Romans 5:3-5

"Behold, we count them happy which endure. Ye have heard of the patience of Job, and have seen the end of the Lord; that the Lord is very pitiful, and of tender mercy."
James 5:11

Notes:

7

Clay Belcher's Fabulous Wheels

When Dad's church in Grapevine, Texas, was in the final building program there was a group of boys in the neighborhood interested in the old Soap Box Derby cars. We did not have any money to build a car to Soap Box Derby specifications, but Dad showed us how to build a simple wooden car to race down the hill.

Bethel Baptist Church in Grapevine is located on Hilltop Drive, and Hilltop is named that for a reason. From the Church going west, Hilltop has a rather steep grade going down to Dove Road. About two thirds of the way down the hill is the parking lot of an old church building.

The boys would go through the scrap pile to find pieces of lumber suitable for a small wooden car. We used pieces of iron rebar for the axles, and old wagon wheels to complete our cars, and then paint them with whatever color we found in the garage, and off to the races we would go.

It was great fun when my turn came to sit in the car and steer with a loop of rope around the front wheels. Starting at the top of the hill by the church, we would push the cars the first few yards to get them going, and then coast down the hill in a race. Since all our cars were all pretty much designed and made with the same materials, the race came down to our skills as a driver.

One day, out of the blue, Clay Belcher came to our races with a car of his own design. Clay was a kid from two blocks away, the outsider as it were. His car was a much lighter design than ours so we were leery of the outcome. The first race was a shock. Clay got a push like the rest of us, then his car raced down the hill before any of us could get half way down! Race after race, against all the different cars we had, Clay was the winner. A few days later we were racing again and Clay showed up. He won every race; His car was that fast.

One time, Clay was distracted for a moment and I went to look at his car. I picked up the rear tires off the ground and gave them a spin. I could hear the click, click, click of the roller bearings inside the wheels. His car was not running like ours on rough iron rebar and old wagon wheels; Clay had acquired some roller bearing wheels which ran on a smooth steel axle. He was not cheating; he just had better equipment. The wheels were a great prize for a young boy racing a wooden car down a hill.

The Bible tells us of a man who found a great prize and what he did about it.

> *"Again, the kingdom of heaven is like unto treasure hid in a field; the which when a man hath found, he hideth, and for joy thereof goeth and selleth all that he hath, and buyeth that field."*
> *Matthew 13:44*

> *"Again, the kingdom of heaven is like unto a merchant man, seeking goodly pearls: Who, when he had found one pearl of great price, went and sold all that he had, and bought it."*

Matthew 13:45-46

The first thing is we need to recognize is the value a great prize of knowing the LORD can be. The Apostle Paul desired nothing but the knowledge of the love of Christ.

> *"That Christ may dwell in your hearts by faith; that ye, being rooted and grounded in love, May be able to comprehend with all saints what is the breadth, and length, and depth, and height; And to know the love of Christ, which passeth knowledge, that ye might be filled with all the fulness of God."*
> *Ephesians 3:17-19*

And again,

> *"Yea doubtless, and I count all things but loss for the excellency of the knowledge of Christ Jesus my Lord: for whom I have suffered the loss of all things, and do count them but dung, that I may win Christ,"*
> *Philippians 3:8*

I did not know how, but I had to acquire some wheels like Clay's. I knew it would not be easy. Clay knew he was the champion of our races, and, since we had no wheels like his, there was no way we could win.

I began to think long and hard on how to trade for those wheels. If we could get Christian people to think as hard on the things of God as I did on those wheels, our churches would really go. It took several offers, a long time, and some of my precious things, but I finally made a deal with Clay for those wheels.

The ecstasy of reward was worth the agony of acquisition. I used those wheels for a long time, eventually making a gasoline powered go-cart which I rode around the neighborhood. I finally had Clay Belcher's fabulous wheels!

ADDITIONAL SCRIPTURES:

"Lay not up for yourselves treasures upon earth, where moth and rust doth corrupt, and where thieves break through and steal: But lay up for yourselves treasures in heaven, where neither moth nor rust doth corrupt, and where thieves do not break through nor steal: For where your treasure is, there will your heart be also."
Matthew 6:19-21

"Sell that ye have, and give alms; provide yourselves bags which wax not old, a treasure in the heavens that faileth not, where no thief approacheth, neither moth corrupteth."
Luke 12:33

"For where your treasure is, there will your heart be also."

Luke 12:34

"Whom have I in heaven but thee? and there is none upon earth that I desire beside thee."
Psalm 73:25

"But it is good for me to draw near to God: I have put my trust in the Lord GOD, that I may declare all thy works."
Psalm 73:28

"My soul fainteth for thy salvation: but I hope in thy word."
Psalm 119:81

Notes:

8

Have You Kissed Any Frogs Today?

Many years ago I heard a simple song which asked: Have you kissed any frogs today? It is not exactly a pleasant idea, but sometimes to help someone it requires doing some things that can be thought of as *unpleasant*.

We all know the story of the princess who kissed the frog and he transformed into a handsome prince. A cute children's fairy tale, but the idea of kissing a frog?

The Bible has the story of the Good Samaritan, where a man helped another who had been hurt. As the story goes, a man was on a journey when he was met by a group of thieves, beat-up, robbed, and left for dead.

Shortly thereafter, a Priest came to him and saw him, and then passed by on the other side of the road. Likewise, a Levite (a man from the Israeli tribe of Levi) came to him, and he also passed by on the other side of the road. Then a man from Samaria came by and had compassion on him. The Samaritan treated the man's wounds, placed him on his animal, and took him to an inn to get a room where he could recover.

Oh, did I mention that the Samaritans were looked down upon by the Jews? Yet this Samaritan man had enough compassion in his being to help someone who might or might not like him.

Every weekday I drive through Pecan Gap on my way to work. On the return trip to Roxton, as I pass through Pecan Gap, I see a sign which says, "Help Somebody Today." The sign is what reminded me of that song.

Recently there was a situation where someone I know was helping another person. Being glad to help, he offered food, housing, and a little monetary assistance. But the situation turned as the one being helped became more demanding. Eventually the situation spiraled out of control to the point where a restraining order was necessary.

Sometimes when we help someone, especially a stranger, we might feel that we are being taken. I have been taken a time or two myself. It will stir a feeling of betrayal and embarrassment, and we wonder if we should help someone again. The answer is yes.

We are not responsible for how someone will use our benevolence, but it is important that we be mindful and wise of the situation. We are to be "wise as serpents and harmless as doves." And who knows, perhaps our acts of kindness will point someone towards Christ.

When I was a kid, my mom could make fried chicken which was out of this world. And what's more, back in those days she would buy a whole chicken and cut it up herself. Mom had a way of cutting up the chicken where the wishbone piece would be fried as well. The wishbone was mine.

Mom also made gravy, potatoes, biscuits, a vegetable, and iced tea for our chicken supper. I don't know how, but the word seemed to get out when mom would fry chicken, and someone would always come to the door asking for food. It only took a heartbeat for Dad to gather up our fried chicken supper and give it to the less fortunate. We kissed a frog.

Then, he would go to the store and buy bologna and bread for our supper. Not an equal to the chicken which just went out the door, but no one complained, as we were there to help people.

There is a risk when you help someone. It is possible you might get taken, but remember that God knows our intentions were pure, and He will bless us for it.

ADDITIONAL SCRIPTURES:

"For the poor shall never cease out of the land: therefore I command thee, saying, Thou shalt open thine hand wide unto thy brother, to thy poor, and to thy needy, in thy land."
Deuteronomy 15:11

"This is my commandment, That ye love one another, as I have loved you."
John 15:12

We then that are strong ought to bear the infirmities of the weak, and not to please ourselves."
Romans 15:1

"Bear ye one another's burdens, and so fulfil the law of Christ."
Galatians 6:2

"Look not every man on his own things, but every man also on the things of others."
Philippians 2:4

"For ye know the grace of our Lord Jesus Christ, that, though he was rich, yet for your sakes he became poor, that ye through his poverty might be rich."
II Corinthians 8:9

Notes:

9

How Now Brown Cow

Isn't it strange that a brown cow can eat green grass, produce white milk, which can be churned into yellow butter? I've never figured out how that works but it does.

God has given man the wisdom and knowledge to husband dairy cows to harvest the milk they produce.

New Christians begin a wonderful journey into the knowledge of Christ by teachings which are basic and easy to grasp. As the Christian grows, the appetite should grow for the meat of the Word of God. This takes time.

Some Christians become stuck with no growth, and as a result are not ready for the meat of the Word of God. There are deeper and more wonderful truths which must be learned in order to grow in the Lord. The Apostle Paul ran into this problem and this is what he said,

> *"I have fed you with milk, and not with meat: for hitherto* (Or up until now) *ye were not able to bear it, neither yet now are ye able. For ye are yet carnal: for whereas there is among you envying, and strife, and divisions, are ye not carnal, and walk as men?"*
> *Corinthians 3:2-3*

This analogy shows us that Christian's need to be weaned from the milk of the Word to show their maturity in the Lord, being yielded to Him and willing to follow His commandments.

Has your pastor recommended a foreign missions program as an outreach of the church? Did you embrace it or resist it?

Do you just sit in the pew and never engage in helping your pastor reach the lost? Do you pray for him or do you forget him until the next Sunday?

If your pastor desires to reach the people of your city with an activity, do you leave all the details up to him, or do you engage and help any way which you can?

I think you can figure out if you have matured as a Christian or not. Those who have not matured from the milk of the Word will only think of themselves.

ADDITIONAL SCRIPTURES:

"For this cause we also, since the day we heard it, do not cease to pray for you, and to desire that ye might be filled with the knowledge of his will in all wisdom and spiritual understanding; That ye might walk worthy of the Lord unto all pleasing, being fruitful in every good work, and increasing in the knowledge of God; Strengthened with all might, according to his glorious power, unto all patience and longsuffering with joyfulness;"
Colossians 1:9-11

"But grow in grace, and in the knowledge of

our Lord and Saviour Jesus Christ. To him be glory both now and forever."
II Peter 3:18

"But speaking the truth in love, may grow up into him in all things, which is the head, even Christ:"
Ephesians 4:15

"Be ye followers of me, even as I also am of Christ."
I Corinthians 11:1

"And let us consider one another to provoke unto love and to good works:"
Hebrews 10:24

Notes:

10

Dealing With an "I" Problem

The LORD God gave commands in the Old Testament to the Children of Israel. These commands are recorded with their results, and the joys of following them or the consequences of disobedience. These are recorded in the Scriptures as an example for our benefit.

Take for example the last king of Judah. His name was Zedekiah.

Now, what is the first great commandment? God specifically pointed this out many years prior to Zedekiah. Had he kept up in the studies of the Scripture he would have known.

"And thou shalt love the LORD thy God with
all thine heart, and with all thy soul, and
with all thy might."
Deuteronomy 6:5

Zedekiah ignored this, and went on to worship the false god Baal.

As king of Judah, he was privy to all the historical records of Judah and Israel. It was known that when the people worshiped idols such as Baal, that God would not give His blessing. Israel many times suffered the consequences of disobedience to God. Zedekiah had to know that Israel suffered greatly when they worshiped Baal. He knew that Elijah the prophet of God prophesied there would be no rain. A drought and famine ensued during the reign of Ahab of Israel.

The Prophet Jeremiah and Zedekiah had many choice words between each other. When Zedekiah sought the Word of the LORD through Jeremiah, Zedekiah did not like the answer. He had an "I" problem because he did not hear what he wanted to hear.

For a little context, Zedekiah was the last King of Judah. Israel was a divided kingdom. The Northern Kingdom of Israel, made up of ten of the tribes of Israel, had fallen into captivity to the Assyrians about two hundred years earlier. The northern kingdom was deep into idolatry. The LORD God said of idols,

"Thou shalt have no other gods before me. Thou shalt not make unto thee any graven image, or any likeness of anything that is in heaven above, or that is in the earth beneath, or that is in the water under the earth. Thou shalt not bow down thyself to them, nor serve them: for I the LORD thy God am a jealous God, visiting the iniquity of the fathers upon the children unto third and fourth generation of them that hate me; And shewing mercy unto thousands of them that love me, and keep my commandments."
Exodus 20:3-6

God is perfectly clear about idolatry. We are not to bow down to worship anything or anyone else except the LORD.

King Zedekiah was a weak and immature king. It is quite possible that he did not know the LORD, only eternity will reveal that truth. He placed his own arrogance and pride ahead of the LORD God, and he paid the price.

King Zedekiah was actually set up as a puppet king by King Nebuchadnezzar of Babylon. Judah had been conquered by King Nebuchadnezzar, and all the treasures of Judah were taken to Babylon. These treasures of gold and other precious things included the literate and skilled people of Judah including a young man by the name of Daniel. Zedekiah was also to pay tribute to King Nebuchadnezzar every year. He did something bold as well as foolish. He rebelled against King Nebuchadnezzar.

After a while, Nebuchadnezzar realized that he had been affronted by Zedekiah, so Nebuchadnezzar put Jerusalem in a siege. For three years nothing went in or out of Jerusalem. It was not long until the stores of food in Jerusalem were exhausted. The people became very hungry. Zedekiah, thinking of himself first, had a real problem.

Zedekiah went to Jeremiah to ask what to do. The LORD told Jeremiah to tell Zedekiah to give up and surrender to the Babylonian army. God said that if they would do as He said, the city of Jerusalem would not be destroyed and the people would live. Of course, that meant more Babylonian captivity.

"And unto this people thou shalt say, Thus saith the LORD; Behold, I set before you the way of life, and the way of death. He that

abideth in this city shall die by the sword,
and by the famine, and by the pestilence:
but he that goeth out, and falleth to the
Chaldeans that besiege you, he shall live,
and his life shall be unto him for a prey."
Jeremiah 21:8-9

Zedekiah did not like those words from the LORD. Therefore, Zedekiah put Jeremiah into prison and treated him roughly. As the siege grew worse and the city ran out of food, he asked Jeremiah once again for the word of the LORD.

"Then said Jeremiah unto Zedekiah, Thus
saith the LORD, the God of hosts, the God of
Israel; If thou wilt assuredly go forth unto
the king of Babylon's princes, then thy soul
shall live, and this city shall not be burned
with fire; and thou shalt live, and thine
house: But if thou wilt not go forth to the
king of Babylon's princes, then shall this city
be given into the hand of the Chaldeans,
and they shall burn it with fire, and thou
shalt not escape out of their hand."
Jeremiah 38:17-18

Zedekiah did not like to hear those words at all. Jeremiah was placed in a dry well as punishment, as if that would make the LORD God change His mind. He placed his trust in idolatry, putting himself first ahead of the LORD, and the city of Jerusalem would pay the price.

Zedekiah knew that to surrender to the Babylonians would mean he would be king of Judah in name only, no power, no authority. God was serious about Zedekiah and Judah's idolatry.

I have seen folks with a serious "I" problem. If the pastor desires to encourage an outreach ministry, they will refuse to participate, especially if offerings are involved. They have not matured in the LORD, not willing to follow His commandments. It is amazing that some of these folks hold positions in the church and then assume an authority not sanctioned by the LORD in His Word.

As the city of Jerusalem ran out of food, the people grew weak from the famine. Eventually the Babylonians overran and burned the city and destroyed the Temple. Zedekiah tried to escape with his sons and other members of the royal court. He was caught and judged by Nebuchadnezzar. Jeremiah recorded the following,

> "But the army of the Chaldeans pursued after the king, and overtook Zedekiah in the plains of Jericho; and all his army was scattered from him. Then they took the king, and carried him up unto the king of Babylon to Riblah in the land of Hamath; where he gave judgment upon him. And the king of Babylon slew the sons of Zedekiah before his eyes: he slew also all the princes of Judah in Riblah. Then he put out the eyes of Zedekiah; and the king of Babylon bound him in chains, and carried him to Babylon, and put him in prison till the

day of his death."
Jeremiah 52:8-11

Zedekiah had an "I" problem all of his reign as king of Judah, and he paid a dear price for his arrogance and pride.

ADDITIONAL SCRIPTURES:

"Look not every man on his own things, but every man also on the things of others."
Philippians 2:4

"For men shall be lovers of their own selves, covetous, boasters, proud, blasphemers, disobedient to parents, unthankful, unholy, without natural affection, trucebreakers, false accusers, incontinent, fierce, despisers of those that are good, Traitors, heady, high-minded, lovers of pleasures more than lovers of God; Having a form of godliness, but denying the power thereof: from such turn away"
II Timothy 3:2-5

"Bear ye one another's burdens, and so fulfil the law of Christ."
Galatians 6:2

"Whoso stoppeth his ears at the cry of the poor, he also shall cry himself, but shall not

be heard."
Proverbs 21:13

"This is my commandment, That ye love one another, as I have loved you."
John 15:12

Notes:

11

It Will Rain Again

I was born in 1954. At the time, west Texas was enduring a drought, to the point that folks were making up jokes to remember the drought. Some go like this:

"It was so dry that we had to attach a postage stamp to an envelope with a paper clip."

"It was so dry the cows gave powdered milk."

"When my son was 21 we saw a rain shower on the horizon, we made sure he saw it because he had never seen rain."

It is natural for parts of the country to be in a drought and other areas to be wet, but if you are in a place either wet or dry, rest assured, it will rain again. The LORD God made promises about rain and seasons of planting and harvest.

"And Noah builded an altar unto the LORD; and took of every clean beast, and of every clean fowl, and offered burnt offerings on the altar. And the LORD smelled a sweet savour; and the LORD said in his heart, I will not again curse the ground any more for man's sake; for the imagination of man's heart is evil from his youth; neither will I

again smite any more everything living, as I
have done. While the earth remaineth,
seedtime and harvest, and cold and heat,
and summer and winter, and day and night
shall not cease."
Genesis 8:20-22

When Noah and his family emerged from the Ark after the flood which God had sent to destroy the earth, God was pleased with Noah's sacrifices. It was then that God promised the earth would continue.

God has made the earth for man and the animals, and God is mindful of the needs of all life, and that we need the blessing of rain for hydration and for food.

God is in control of the weather. He pointed this out to Job in the Bible,

"Who hath divided a watercourse for the
overflowing of waters, or a way for the
lightning of thunder; To cause it to rain on
the earth, where no man is; on the
wilderness, wherein there is no man; To
satisfy the desolate and waste ground; and
to cause the bud of the tender herb to
spring forth? Hath the rain a father? or who
hath begotten the drops of dew? Out of
whose womb came the ice? and the hoary
frost of heaven, who hath gendered it? The
waters are hid as with a stone, and the face
of the deep is frozen."
Job 38:25-30

Further, God said this of the lightning,

*"Canst thou lift up thy voice to the clouds,
that abundance of waters may cover thee?
Canst thou send lightnings, that they may
go and say unto thee, Here we are?"*
Job 38:34-35

Of course Job could not command rain or lightning, and neither can we. We are at God's mercy and love for His blessing of rain. God not only rains on us, but He sends rain into the desolate places that the flowers might bloom. Even though we are not there, the flowers and all creation is giving praise to our Creator God.

Rain is crucial to life on earth. God is very well aware of our need for rain, for our crops and our cattle. However, when we sin, God can withhold the rain to remind us that He is the Creator.

In the Bible is the story of King Ahab and the Prophet Elijah. King Ahab was a very wicked king to Israel, leading them further into idolatry. Ahab had married Jezebel, the daughter of the king of Zidon, to further his grip on power. He had forgotten God, worshiped the idol Baal, and actually promoted idol worship in all Israel. God had enough. So God had a remarkable prophet named Elijah, a rough man from the area of Tisbeh in Gilead. Somehow, Elijah gained entrance into Ahab's court and pronounced that it would not rain except by his word. I believe Elijah was very well aware of the law in Deuteronomy,

*"Take heed to yourselves, that your heart be
not deceived, and ye turn aside, and serve
other gods, and worship them; And then the
LORD's wrath be kindled against you, and
he shut up the heaven, that there be no
rain, and that the land yield not her fruit;
and lest ye perish quickly from off the good
land which the LORD giveth you."*
Deuteronomy 11:16-17

I believe that Elijah was absolutely convinced in his heart that God is alive, and that God would fulfill His Word. Elijah also declared that he worshiped the LORD God, and that it would not rain until Elijah said so.

Immediately, a bounty was put on the head of Elijah, and he was instructed by God to spend some time by the brook Cherith. There Elijah drank from the brook and was fed by the ravens. Because of the drought, the brook eventually dried up, and then God had Elijah go to the care of a widow in Zarapath.

When the time was right (after three and a half years) Elijah showed himself to Ahab for a challenge between God and Baal. Of course, Baal is a false god, and idol, dead like those who made him. The challenge was to have a sacrifice whose fire came from heaven by the living God. The prophets of Baal agreed to the challenge against Elijah.

The prophets of Baal went first. They called to Baal all morning and afternoon. Nothing happened. After they gave up, Elijah went next. He rebuilt his altar and arranged the sacrifice in the proper order. He then ordered the sacrifice completely drenched in water. This way there was no natural possibility of fire coming to the sacrifice except of God. Elijah then prayed a 63-word prayer of praise to God. He never asked for fire, but at the conclusion of his prayer, God sent fire from heaven, consumed the sacrifice, the wood, stones the altar was constructed with, the dust, and the water which drenched the sacrifice!

Elijah prayed again, and it rained.

ADDITIONAL SCRIPTURES:

"He answered and said unto them, when it is evening, ye say, It will be fair weather: for the sky is red. And in the morning, It will be foul weather today: for the sky is red and lowring. O ye hypocrites, ye can discern the face of the sky; but can ye not discern the signs of the times?"
Matthew 16:2-3

"Then I will give you rain in due season, and the land shall yield her increase, and the trees of the field shall yield their fruit."
Leviticus 26:4

"The LORD is slow to anger, and great in power, and will not at all acquit the wicked: the LORD hath his way in the whirlwind and in the storm, and the clouds are the dust of

his feet."
Nahum 1:3

*"Elias (Elijah) was a man subject to like
passions as we are, and he prayed earnestly
that it might not rain: and it rained not on
the earth by the space of three years and six
months.*
James 5:17

*"Out of the south cometh the whirlwind:
and cold out of the north."*
Job 37:9

*"But the LORD sent out a great wind into
the sea, and there was a mighty tempest in
the sea, so that the ship was like to be
broken."*
Jonah 1:4

Notes:

12

Kicking the Can Down the Road

Have you ever procrastinated on anything? Especially something that required immediate action?

There is talk these days of many things the Congress of the United States needs to address, but there is no action. They call that "kicking the can down the road." Let someone else make the decision, or I will make the decision later.

When I was a kid I remember having to receive an occasional booster shot for my immunizations. I had a real serious fear of doctors in those days, and I would do anything to postpone the inevitable. I really wanted to kick the can down the road on that. However, I would be taken to the doctor and my immunizations would be caught up with another booster shot, and then I was done.

When it comes to spiritual things, many folks have a hard time making a decision. The Apostle Paul was before King Agrippa telling him about Jesus Christ, but Agrippa was not willing to make a decision for the Lord.

"King Agrippa, believest thou the prophets? I know that thou believest. Then Agrippa said unto Paul, almost thou persuadest me to be a Christian. And Paul said, I would to God, that not only thou, but also all that hear me this day, were both almost, and altogether such as I am, except these

bonds."
Acts 26:27-29

King Agrippa would not accept Christ at that time. Perhaps he was willing to make a decision later. I do not know if Agrippa invited Jesus Christ into his heart at a later date, but his time to decide the day he heard the Gospel.

"(For he saith, I have heard thee in a time
accepted, and in the day of salvation have I
succoured thee: behold, now is the accepted
time; behold, now is the day of salvation.)"
II Corinthians 6:2

Now is the time to get involved with your church. Now is the time to begin reading your Bible. Now is the time to start a prayer life with the Lord. Now is the time to support your pastor. Now is the time to begin tithing. Now is the time to read the Bible to your children at bedtime. Now is the time to give an offering above and beyond the tithe to the LORD.

"The soul of the sluggard desireth, and hath
nothing: but the soul of the diligent shall be
made fat."
Proverbs 13:4

There are rewards for taking action to make a decision.

"But seek ye first the kingdom of God, and his righteousness; and all these things shall be added unto you."
Matthew 6:33

I don't know where you are in your Christian life right now, but I pray that you are growing in the LORD. I pray that you have decided to follow Jesus, no turning back.

ADDITIONAL SCRIPTURES:

"The sluggard will not plow by reason of the cold; therefore, shall he beg in harvest, and have nothing."
Proverbs 20:4

"Boast not thyself of tomorrow; for thou knowest not what a day may bring forth."
Proverbs 27:1

"And he said unto another, Follow me. But he said, Lord, suffer me first to go and bury my father. Jesus said unto him, Let the dead bury their dead: but go thou and preach the kingdom of God. And another also said, Lord, I will follow thee; but let me first go bid them farewell, which are at home at my house. And Jesus said unto him, no man, having put his hand to the plough, and looking back, is fit for the kingdom of God."

Luke 9:59-62

"Be ye therefore ready also: for the Son of man cometh at an hour when ye think not."
Luke 12:40

"Whatsoever thy hand findeth to do, do it with thy might; for there is no work, nor device, nor knowledge, nor wisdom, in the grave, whither thou goest."
Ecclesiastes 9:10

"He that observeth the wind shall not sow; and he that regardeth the clouds shall not reap."
Ecclesiastes 11:4

Notes:

13

Leaving My Sister at the Church

It is probably the dream of every little boy, to leave his younger sister someplace! Well, it happened to our family long ago when we left my little sister at the church.

Jeanne was probably three years old and was very used to life at the church. We went every time the doors were open.

My parents were very involved, and we usually had a carload of people whom we took to and from church with us. At times our car was so full that Jeanne and I were simply on our own. We would squeeze into the car among all the other people for a ride home.

We attended Baptist Temple in Grand Prairie, Texas, a new church started by a pastor named Burt Rutter. The church had grown to the point that a new facility was necessary, and one was built. The memory is so old; the images are a ghostly gray. I do remember the brick planters which were on the front of the church building.

Church was over, and the car was loaded to return our visitors to their homes. Each person was dropped off at his house, and then we went home. Mom took an inventory of the children. We were missing one...Jeanne! Where is she?

This was kind of like the scriptures where Joseph and Mary left Jesus at the Temple. In Luke chapter 2 and verses 42-47 it says,

"And when he was twelve years old, they went up to Jerusalem after the custom of the feast. And when they had fulfilled the days, as they returned, the child Jesus tarried behind in Jerusalem; and Joseph and his mother knew not of it. But they, supposing him to have been in the company, went a day's journey; and they sought him among their kinsfolk and acquaintance. And when they found him not, they turned back again to Jerusalem, seeking him. And it came to pass, that after three days they found him in the temple, sitting in the midst of the doctors, both hearing them, and asking them questions. And all that heard him were astonished at his understanding and answers."

Joseph and Mary just assumed that Jesus was traveling with them and their company; instead, Jesus was at the temple, hearing and asking questions. I don't know why Jesus stayed behind; the Bible doesn't say, but He was there never the less. We do know that Jesus said to Mary and Joseph later that He "must be about my Father's business..."

Jesus had made several trips to Jerusalem before, and He was learning the disciplines of the Temple. There were probably provisions available for those who had to travel from out of town to the Temple. I would imagine that Jesus knew exactly where everything was that He might need.

Even at the young age of twelve, Jesus was the Christ, the Word made flesh. And as sovereign of all things, He knew His destiny. Jesus knew His earthly parents would seek for Him after they were part-way home.

We immediately made a return trip to the church, and, as we got there, we met Pastor Rutter just leaving the church to bring Jeanne home. As he was checking the doors, he found her sitting on the steps of the platform in the front of the church, patiently waiting for someone to take her to lunch. Jeanne knew that everything was all right. Her parents would be back at the church soon.

Children need to be in Church to learn about Jesus and His love for them. They the confidence instilled in them that when they are at the church, everything is okay. Wisdom and understanding about living are available there, just for them.

> *"Train up a child in the way he should go:*
> *and when he is old, he will not depart from*
> *it."*
> *Proverbs 22:6*

I couldn't explain it any better.

ADDITIONAL SCRIPTURES:

> *"The rod and reproof give wisdom: but a child*
> *left to himself bringeth his mother to shame."*
> *Proverbs 29:15*

"And these words, which I command thee this day, shall be in thine heart: And thou shalt teach them diligently unto thy children, and shalt talk of them when thou sittest in thine house, and when thou walkest by the way, and when thou liest down, and when thou risest up."
Deuteronomy 6:6-7

"Lo, children are an heritage of the LORD: and the fruit of the womb is his reward."
Psalm 127:3

"But Jesus said, Suffer little children, and forbid them not, to come unto me: for of such is the kingdom of heaven."
Matthew 19:14

"Chasten thy son while there is hope, and let not thy soul spare for his crying."
Proverbs 19:18

"Correct thy son, and he shall give thee rest; yea, he shall give delight unto thy soul."
Proverbs 29:17

Just a note: I do not advocate any form of child abuse. All discipline should be appropriate for the child and done with love. –Bro. Louis

Notes:

14

Mrs. Daley's Beets

My mother would pick up a couple of widow ladies and bring them to church every Sunday morning. One of those ladies was Mrs. Daley. She and I had a friendship, and we would chat about what was going on in our lives. She found out that I had a small garden and then asked me if I had beets in my garden. I had onions, tomatoes, okra, beans, and some squash, but no beets. She told me she really liked fresh beets.

I went to the store and found some beet seeds. Then I went to my garden and made another row, and planted the beets. After I added a little water, I waited to see what would happen. After all, I was doing something I had never done before; I planted beets. And I really didn't like them!

One thing that God will do is use you in a way where you are not qualified. I knew nothing about beets, but I was planting them for Mrs. Daley. Why is it that God might have put on your heart for you to do something you know nothing about?

God had chosen Moses to lead the Children of Israel out of Egypt. Moses was raised in the palace of Pharaoh and knew the ways of the court. He knew very little about the desert and how to survive. God chose him in spite of his protest to God about being poor of speech and not having any signs where he was sent of God.

Moses still yielded himself to God to deliver the Children of Israel from Egyptian bondage. It was not easy.

God told Moses that the Pharaoh would continually harden his heart, changing his mind about freeing the slaves. But in all ten plagues which came upon Egypt, the LORD God was to be honored and praised.

Well, after a few days, the beets began to sprout. Each Sunday morning, I would give Mrs. Daley an update on her beets. After a few weeks she had me pull a small bunch for her to check out. Thereafter, I pulled beets for her until the growing season for beets was over.

I was successful doing something I had never done before, and frankly would not have done except someone had asked me.

ADDITIONAL SCRIPTURES:

"A new commandment I give unto you, that ye love one another; as I have loved you, that ye also love one another.
John 13:34

"It is like a grain of mustard seed, which a man took, and cast into his garden; and it grew, and waxed a great tree; and the fowls of the air lodged in the branches of it."
Luke 13:19

"Another parable put he forth unto them, saying, The kingdom of heaven is like to a grain of mustard seed, which a man took, and sowed in his field:"
Matthew 13:31

"And the LORD shall guide thee continually, and satisfy thy soul in drought, and make fat thy bones: and thou shalt be like a watered garden, and like a spring of water, whose waters fail not."
Isaiah 58:11

"For as the earth bringeth forth her bud, and as the garden causeth the things that are sown in it to spring forth; so the Lord GOD will cause righteousness and praise to spring forth before all the nations."
Isaiah 61:11

"And they shall say, This land that was desolate is become like the garden of Eden; and the waste and desolate and ruined cities are become fenced, and are inhabited."
Ezekiel 36:35

Notes:

15

One More Night with the Frogs

God had chosen Moses to lead the Israelites out of bondage in the land of Egypt. The king of Egypt, known as the Pharaoh, refused to free the Israelite slaves; thus a contest of wills began between the Pharaoh and God.

In all of this God told Moses that it would be by a strong hand and an outstretched arm of God that the Hebrews would go free. God's people had been slaves in Egypt, and God would not allow His people to leave the land as paupers. Israel would be vindicated.

There were various plagues on the land of Egypt as a result of this stubborn Pharaoh. One of the plagues was a plague of frogs...lots of frogs. Those poor Egyptians had frogs everywhere! In the house, in the food, in the barn, in the water, in the bed...there were frogs everywhere! There was no place to escape the frogs.

The Egyptian people had already suffered the previous plague of the water turned to blood. For a while there, the Egyptian people had to do without water. And now the frogs. Little did the population of Egypt know that there were eight more plagues to deal with, each one getting worse than the one before it!

The stubborn Pharaoh finally called Moses and asked him to call on God to take the frogs away. When Moses asked the Pharaoh when he wanted the frogs taken away, the Pharaoh said "tomorrow!" Personally I would have asked for them to be removed immediately!

I believe that deep down people know they need

to be in a relationship now with God but would rather put it off until "tomorrow" so they can hold out *one more night*. Why put off until tomorrow what you can do today?

God addresses the issue like this,

> *"For he saith, I have heard thee in a time*
> *accepted, and in the day of salvation have I*
> *succoured thee: behold, now is the accepted*
> *time; behold, now is the day of salvation."*
> *II Corinthians 6:2*

Our lives are so fragile. We are but one heartbeat and one breath away from death. To put off what we should do now regarding eternal matters is not wise.

If you have been thinking of getting back in church, now is the time. If you have been thinking about reading your Bible, now is the time. If you are lost in sin and without Christ, now is the time.

Don't procrastinate. Don't put it off. Act now!

ADDITIONAL SCRIPTURES:

> *"Boast not thyself of tomorrow; for thou*
> *knowest not what a day may bring forth."*
> *Proverbs 27:1*

> *"He that observeth the wind shall not sow;*
> *and he that regardeth the clouds shall not*
> *reap."*
> *Ecclesiastes 11:4*

"Be ye therefore ready also: for the Son of man cometh at an hour when ye think not."
Luke 12:40

"The sluggard will not plow by reason of the cold; therefore shall he beg in harvest, and have nothing."
Proverbs 20:4

"He becometh poor that dealeth with a slack hand: but the hand of the diligent maketh rich."
Proverbs 10:4

Notes:

16

Taking Out the Trash

When I was about nine years old, my dad decided I should take part in the weekly ritual of taking the trash out to the road for pick up. I suppose nine is a good age to begin teaching a kid that kind of responsibility, but at the time I didn't think so.

We lived in the parsonage located behind the church building, so the house was a long way from the road. Combined with the weight of the trash cans and the distance from the house to the road, I admit it was difficult to be enthusiastic about my new-found responsibility to the family. Further, back in those days, there was no such thing as plastic trash bags. In place of the plastic bags, my mom would line the kitchen trash can with newspaper to absorb the offending elements in the trash.

During warm weather the trash in the cans outside would have time to get "ripe," if you know what I mean! Finally, to add insult to injury, our trash cans were just -, trash cans. We never had the lids, the cans were beat up and dented, and the bottoms were rusted out. It took a certain kind of humility to put our trash cans on display at the road for all to see!

The Bible says in First Corinthians chapter 6, verses 19 and 20 that our bodies are the temple of the Holy Spirit, and that we have been bought with a price...we belong to God. This thought is humbling. Makes a person want to clean up and get rid of the trash. God does not want you to put it on display; He said that He would take the issues in your life…the trash… and remove them as far as the east is from the west.

> *"As far as the east is from the west, so far hath he removed our transgressions from us."*
> *Psalm 103:12*

Think about that. If you were to go east around the world, you would never meet the west! Wow! Once God removes it, it's removed forever!

> *"Who is a God like unto thee, that pardoneth iniquity, and passeth by the transgression of the remnant of his heritage? he retaineth not his anger forever, because he delighteth in mercy."*
> *Micah 7:18*

God is marvelous as He patiently waits for us to come to Him! There is a word you will hear in church services every once in a while, "Longsuffering." It means that God is exercising a joyous patience for us to return to Him. He takes great joy when we give Him the issues in our lives and trust Him with them.

A few years later the church bought another house across the street from the church as the parsonage. We moved over there with great joy. I think those old trash cans moved with us. At least the trip to the road was a lot shorter.

ADDITIONAL SCRIPTURES:

"I, even I, am he that blotteth out thy transgressions for mine own sake, and will not remember thy sins."
Isaiah 43:25

"For I will be merciful to their unrighteousness, and their sins and their iniquities will I remember no more."
Hebrews 8:12

"This is the covenant that I will make with them after those days, saith the Lord, I will put my laws into their hearts, and in their minds will I write them; And their sins and iniquities will I remember no more."
Hebrews 10:16-17

"For this is the covenant that I will make with the house of Israel after those days, saith the Lord; I will put my laws into their mind, and write them in their hearts: and I will be to them a God, and they shall be to me a people:"
Hebrews 8:10

"This I say then, Walk in the Spirit, and ye shall not fulfil the lust of the flesh."
Galatians 5:16

"Let not sin therefore reign in your mortal body, that ye should obey it in the lusts thereof."
Romans 6:12

Notes:

17

When Things are not as They Appear

Dad told me the story about when he and one of the men of the church went fishing. Raymond Richardson and his wife Leona lived close to the church, and there was an occasion when he and dad went fishing in a boat; Leona and Mom stayed on the shore of the lake to fish as well.

It so happened that, on this day, the sand bass were "schooling," making them easy to catch. They call it "schooling" when the sand bass come to the top of the water in a feeding frenzy, apparently mad with hunger. They will bite at anything shiny like a small bait fish, the shad, or a shiny artificial lure.

Dad and Raymond caught a full stringer of fish and brought them to the shore where Mom and Leona were camped, then went back out on the lake for more fishing. Leona had set up a table for cleaning the fish on the spot, and Mom was close by with a cane pole fishing with minnows.

Leona had quite an operation going cleaning all those fish. About that time, a car load of want-a-be fishers drove into their day camp. And suddenly, Mom caught a fish on the cane pole and screamed as she pulled the fish out of the water!

To the amazement of the people in the car, they watched as Leona took the fish from Mom's cane pole and baited it again with another minnow. Then Leona began cleaning that fish along with the others on the table. It appeared that Mom had caught all those fish! The folks in the car became very excited about fishing.

There are many deceptions in the world, all intended to deceive you into believing there is something else there instead of what you see.

The Scriptures tell us that the devil will tempt us three different ways. You might say it is "old school" because the devil has not changed his tactics much. In First John 2:16 it says,

> *"For all that is in the world, the lust of the flesh, and the lust of the eyes, and the pride of life, is not of the Father, but is of the world."*

If you think about it, we humans are *in the flesh* and vulnerable to fleshly temptation. We see it all the time as it has permeated our society. Advertisers will use sex to sell many of their wares. That is the lust of the flesh.

The devil also tempts us by what we see. Don't those new cars look good on television? How about those girls at the beach party? How about the dude in the new hot car? Yep, that's the lust of the eyes.

The pride of life gets closer to home. It involves your person and your position. Money, riches, and personal well-being are on the list.

We must be careful as many things presented to us by the world are not what they appear to be. There is always some loophole or detail which diminishes what is presented. And that is the advantage of keeping God and the Lord Jesus Christ at the center of our lives. We are safe and secure in Him, and everything is perfectly clear.

ADDITIONAL SCRIPTURES:

"Beloved, believe not every spirit, but try the spirits whether they are of God: because many false prophets are gone out into the world."
I John 4:1

"But evil men and seducers shall wax worse and worse, deceiving, and being deceived."
II Timothy 3:13

"Put on the whole armour of God, that ye may be able to stand against the wiles of the devil."
Ephesians 6:11

"And the great dragon was cast out, that old serpent, called the Devil, and Satan, which deceiveth the whole world: he was cast out into the earth, and his angels were cast out with him."
Revelation 12:9

"Nor thieves, nor covetous, nor drunkards, nor revilers, nor extortioners, shall inherit the kingdom of God."
I Corinthians 6:10

*"Ye shall not steal, neither deal falsely,
neither lie one to another."*
Leviticus 19:11

Notes:

18

To Be Forever Young

There have been times in my life when I learned something extraordinary and then commented "If I had only learned that when I was younger!" Those are special "Aha!" moments- life moments when you realize what you have wasted since your youth. If only we could turn back the clock to reclaim what was lost. If only to be young once again.

Man is a creation of God who inhabits the dimension we call time. It is God who inhabits the dimension called Eternity. God is not bound by eternity or time because He is equally present in both. God is also all-knowing, meaning that He knows every detail of every life on this earth. That includes lives in the past, the present, and the future. God also loves us, so He gave us his written Word, the Bible, as a guide to living life. It contains the very words of God so the Bible is completely accurate and reliable.

If young men and women would read and learn from the Word of God, then lives could be lived with greater joy and peace. God desires our lives to be abundant and full.

Perhaps you too have experienced moments when something remarkable is learned and then comment to yourself about wishing you had learned it when you were young.

Why not start living young again?

It was Solomon who wrote in Ecclesiastes 12:1,

"Remember now thy Creator in the days of thy youth."

If you are advanced in your years you can restore spiritual youth by remembering the LORD God. David wrote these words in Psalm 71:5,

"For thou art my hope, O Lord GOD: thou art my trust from my youth."

Jesus was speaking with the woman at the well in John chapter 4 and He called salvation a "well of living water, springing up to life eternal." Restore the joy of your salvation, and start young and fresh once again.

ADDITIONAL SCRIPTURES:

"His flesh shall be fresher than a child's: he shall return to the days of his youth:"
Job 33:25

"Bless the LORD, O my soul, and forget not all his benefits: Who forgiveth all thine iniquities; who healeth all thy diseases; Who redeemeth thy life from destruction; who crowneth thee with lovingkindness and tender mercies; Who satisfieth thy mouth with good things; so that thy youth is renewed like the eagle's."
Psalm 103:2-5

"That our sons may be as plants grown up in their youth; that our daughters may be as corner stones, polished after the similitude of a palace:"
Psalm 144:12

"O God, thou hast taught me from my youth: and hitherto have I declared thy wondrous works."
Psalm 71:17

"Now also when I am old and grayheaded, O God, forsake me not; until I have shewed thy strength unto this generation, and thy power to every one that is to come."
Psalm 71:18

Notes:

19

The Value of What You Don't Know

Six Flags Over Texas opened in Arlington Texas in the mid-1960's. About a year after it opened, a family in Dad's church took me with them on a family outing. Back then, Six Flags was more historical in nature to the six different political flags which once flew over the Lone Star State.

One of the rides at the park back then was the French River Boat, where guests would sit in a boat that navigated its way through hostile animals and Indians on the attack. What was so funny, is that our host on the ride was pointing out the adventure and then would tell us to duck down when the Indians attacked so we wouldn't get an arrow. When the announcement was made, I obediently got out of my seat and ducked down low. To my amazement, I was the only one to duck!

The family which took me to the park later explained to me the ride and how the Indians were not real, and neither were the wild animals. They told me that the next time the host told us to duck, it was okay to remain in my seat and enjoy the show. I agreed.

A little later in the afternoon, I wanted to ride the French River Boat once again to prove my bravery. As the boat again navigated its way through the adventure, I did not flinch when the fake alligators came toward the boat. I sat proudly as the Indians came out to the bank to shoot their arrows.   Best of all, I lived through the adventure!

It's a fact that no one knows everything. There's a

lot to learn out there in our ever changing world, and sometimes we feel overwhelmed by it all. Some things we should learn, but many other things might not be worth the effort to learn. The trick for each of us is to discern the things that we should learn and ignore those things deemed not worth learning. Unfortunately, things not worth learning are often marketed with an attraction which is difficult to resist.

For example, our society is obsessed with learning all there is to know about celebrities. As evidence I submit the pre-occupation with the lives of celebrities found in magazines at most grocery checkouts and the internet. People are drawn to the glitz and glamour of the lives which celebrities live. The truth be told, your life would move right along just fine without this information; therefore, there must not be much value in the learning.

Jesus desires we learn of Him...He said in Matthew 11:29,

"Take my yoke upon you, and learn of me;
for I am meek and lowly in heart: and ye
shall find rest unto your souls."

This is an interesting paradox. A yoke is used by oxen to pull a cart or a plow, and Jesus wants us to wear His "yoke."

The oxen would be harnessed to the yoke and would learn the way of their master as they pulled a plow or cart. The more they wore the yoke the more they learned the task commanded by their lord.

God also said in Psalm chapter 55:22,

"Cast thy burden upon the LORD, and he shall sustain thee: he shall never suffer the righteous to be moved."

In order to wear the yoke of Jesus Christ, we must give Him our burdens. Jesus does not want us to be weighed down with burdens we cannot carry, but to give them to Him. The burden of the yoke of Jesus is much lighter than the yoke the world would harness around us.

Sometimes we learn something enlightening which will encourage us to learn more. There is that *"Ah-ha"* moment when we discover there is much more which *needs* to be learned. It's that need which makes us realize there are things we don't know but would be valuable to us, once learned.

ADDITIONAL SCRIPTURES:

"A wise man will hear, and will increase learning; and a man of understanding shall attain unto wise counsels:"
Proverbs 1:5

"The fear of the LORD is the beginning of knowledge: but fools despise wisdom and instruction."
Proverbs 1:7

"Whoso loveth instruction loveth knowledge: but he that hateth reproof is

brutish."
Proverbs 12:1

"Thou through thy commandments hast made me wiser than mine enemies: for they are ever with me. I have more understanding than all my teachers: for thy testimonies are my meditation. I understand more than the ancients, because I keep thy precepts."
Psalm 119:98-100

"And what nation is there so great, that hath statutes and judgments so righteous as all this law, which I set before you this day?"
Deuteronomy 4:8

"Wherefore the law is holy, and the commandment holy, and just, and good."
Romans 7:12

Notes:

20

Unbelief in the Power of Prayer

There is the old joke about the congregation which found out a bar was being built across the street from the church. The congregation joined together in prayer, asking God to intervene to prevent the bar from opening. A few days before the bar was to open, a violent thunderstorm came through and lightning struck the new building, burning it completely to the ground.

The next day it was difficult for the church congregation to contain their joy; it was obvious that God heard and answered their prayers. Their joy was short-lived however, when the church was served with papers where the owner of the bar was suing them for his loss. In court, the church vehemently denied the accusation. The judge, bewildered, announced he did not know how to rule in this case. He said "It is clear that we have the owner of a bar which believes in the power of prayer, and a church congregation that doesn't!"

The reality today is that many churches have lost their power due to the lack of prayer. Prayer is the gift from God that allows us to communicate with Him. He has given us The Word of God, the Bible, and we pray back to Him in fellowship sweet.

Seems almost anything can keep people from their prayer life- family, friends, or a show on television. When we give prayer a low priority in our lives it usually doesn't happen. Then the devil has gained a victory as we become spiritually anemic and weak.

The truth is, fervent prayer is a lot of work. You have to carve time out of your day, make it a priority, and then spend time with God. You might be a person of a few words, and that is okay. God knew there would be times that we are short on words. It is perfectly all right and honorable to use the Word of God in your prayers. The next time you are short on words, open your Bible to Psalm 23, read it out loud back to the LORD, and then thank Him for the promise of His care as outlined in the Psalm. You see, God already knows about your aches and pains, and He already knows about your relative which might have cancer. What God really desires is that you would take precious time out of your day to honor and praise Him. It is good to ask God to work in the lives of people dealing with disease, for He cares greatly about them. Just remember to praise Him, for *there* is the power of prayer.

ADDITIONAL SCRIPTURES:

"Be careful for nothing; but in everything by prayer and supplication with thanksgiving let your requests be made known unto God."
Philippians 4:6

"Continue in prayer, and watch in the same with thanksgiving;"
Colossians 4:2

"The sacrifice of the wicked is an

abomination to the LORD: but the prayer of the upright is his delight."
Proverbs 15:8

"Praying always with all prayer and supplication in the Spirit, and watching thereunto with all perseverance and supplication for all saints;"
Ephesians 6:18

"These all continued with one accord in prayer and supplication, with the women, and Mary the mother of Jesus, and with his brethren"
Acts 1:14

"Pray without ceasing."
I Thessalonians 5:17

Notes:

21

An Admission of Inadequacy

When I was a much younger man, there wasn't anything that I wouldn't tackle to get the job done. I overhauled engines, remodeled houses, did plumbing work, and made numerous repairs to just about everything. I was truly a jack-of-all-trades.

I would fix the lawnmower, the kids' bicycles, the car, the house, even my mother-in-law's mobile home. In all of this, there would be something happen which I could not fix.

It was around 1995 that my lovely wife started having a severe numbness and tingling in her hands, legs, and feet. She described it like the feeling you have when your foot goes to "sleep." At one point, the numbness moved up her legs and made its way to her waist.

We went to our family doctor, and he ran a battery of tests. Everything was negative. He then referred us to a neurologist. Again, another round of testing was done and we waited impatiently for the results. We made the trip back to the neurologist only to find out that Jan had Multiple Sclerosis. By then the numbness which was up to her waist had receded back down her legs to just below her knees.

I was heartbroken, for now Jan had something I could not fix. For the first time in my life I felt very inadequate. When she had a cold or the flu I would take her soups and soda, and when she had a headache, I would take her pain relievers. But with the MS there was nothing I could do.

When Solomon assumed the throne from his father David in Jerusalem, he knew that there was much he did not know about governing a people. Solomon approached God, then God answered him,

> "In that night did God appear unto Solomon, and said unto him, Ask what I shall give thee. And Solomon said unto God, Thou hast shewed great mercy unto David my father, and hast made me to reign in his stead. Now, O LORD God, let thy promise unto David my father be established: for thou hast made me king over a people like the dust of the earth in multitude. Give me now wisdom and knowledge, that I may go out and come in before this people: for who can judge this thy people, that is so great?"
> II Chronicles 1:7-10

Solomon's request was out of the ordinary, for all the kings who followed Solomon never asked for wisdom and understanding to govern their people. God honored Solomon's request, and not only gave him wisdom, but riches beyond any monarch who has ever lived. His admission of inadequacy to God allowed God to bless him in ways he could not dream.

The adventure with Jan and her MS has been interesting for me. There really isn't much I can do for the MS. I do watch that I don't over-do things, allowing Jan the dignity of keeping her house and engaging in the things of interest to her. I allow her to fuss at me when I don't pick up my socks, obediently acknowledging with a loving "Yes Ma'am". Many of the crafts that Jan will do is a blessing to our ministry here in Roxton, as each and every birthday and anniversary card we send out is hand made by her.

Jan is loved by all the folks at First Baptist Church in Roxton, and she is my greatest asset.

ADDITIONAL SCRIPTURES:

"Therefore I take pleasure in infirmities, in reproaches, in necessities, in persecutions, in distresses for Christ's sake: for when I am weak, then am I strong."
II Corinthians 12:10

"Fear thou not; for I am with thee: be not dismayed; for I am thy God: I will strengthen thee; yea, I will help thee; yea, I will uphold thee with the right hand of my righteousness."
Isaiah 41:10

"After these things the word of the LORD came unto Abram in a vision, saying, Fear not, Abram: I am thy shield, and thy exceeding great reward."
Genesis 15:1

"I can do all things through Christ which

strengtheneth me."
Philippians 4:13

*"Being confident of this very thing, that he
which hath begun a good work in you will
perform [it] until the day of Jesus Christ:"*
Philippians 1:6

*"For God hath not given us the spirit of fear;
but of power, and of love, and of a sound
mind."*
II Timothy 1:7

Notes:

22

Association Begets Assimilation

Perhaps you have heard it said "birds of a feather flock together." That is true, you become like who you run with. So, association begets assimilation.

Many years ago I heard, "I don't cuss, drink, smoke, or chew, and I don't run with those that do." Rest assured, you will become like the people you run with. So tell me, who do you run with?

God gave man the gift of choice, meaning that he can decide for himself what he wants to be, or whom he desires to hang around with. In other words, God does not have a string attached to man, forcing him one way or another. He desires that you follow Him, and that you love Him freely, on your own. God desires that you would choose for yourself to leave behind the trappings of this world which is so predominate today.

"That ye put off concerning the former conversation the old man, which is corrupt according to the deceitful lusts; And be renewed in the spirit of your mind; And that ye put on the new man, which after God is created in righteousness and true holiness."
Ephesians 4:22-24

Further, the Apostle Paul described more details about the changing of your mind,

"Wherefore putting away lying, speak every man truth with his neighbour: for we are members one of another. Be ye angry, and sin not: let not the sun go down upon your wrath: Neither give place to the devil. Let him that stole steal no more: but rather let him labour, working with his hands the thing which is good, that he may have to give to him that needeth. Let no corrupt communication proceed out of your mouth, but that which is good to the use of edifying, that it may minister grace unto the hearers. And grieve not the Holy Spirit of God, whereby ye are sealed unto the day of redemption. Let all bitterness, and wrath, and anger, and clamour, and evil speaking, be put away from you, with all malice:"
Ephesians 4:25-31

This is great! These things mentioned by Paul are opposites of thinking in this world. Seek truth and abandon lying, because we are all one community, and then we are told to resolve our anger the same day we get mad. Ouch! I see men who hang on to their anger, hoping for that exact moment of revenge. And now Paul addresses theft, cursing, bitterness, wrath, anger, clamor, and finally evil speaking. Different from cursing, that could be plain old gossiping about folks.

Finally, Paul taught us how to think rightly, and make good choices about friends.

"And be ye kind one to another, tenderhearted, forgiving one another, even as God for Christ's sake hath forgiven you."
Ephesians 4:32

I don't know who your friends are, but you do. If they don't encourage you in the way of the LORD, perhaps it is time to re-evaluate who you hang out with.

ADDITIONAL SCRIPTURES:

"A froward man soweth strife: and a whisperer separateth chief friends."
Proverbs 16:28

"But whoso hath this world's good, and seeth his brother have need, and shutteth up his bowels of compassion from him, how dwelleth the love of God in him?"
I John 3:17

"A friend loveth at all times, and a brother is born for adversity."
Proverbs 17:17

"Greater love hath no man than this, that a man lay down his life for his friends."
John 15:13

"A man [that hath] friends must shew

himself friendly: and there is a friend [that]
sticketh closer than a brother."
Proverbs 18:24

"Wherefore comfort yourselves together,
and edify one another, even as also ye do."
I Thessalonians 5:11

Notes:

23

It's Not Just a Piece of Paper

Part of the responsibilities of being a pastor is officiating at funerals and weddings. I have been in the ministry as a bi-vocational pastor for about four years, and I have preached six funerals and officiated at only one wedding. If something doesn't change soon, we will all be in trouble.

I meet a lot of happy young couples with children, but they are not married. They are functioning as a family, the kids go to school, and they are materially successful. It would seem that all is right.

Marriage is established of God. He commanded that a man and a woman would make a commitment to each other and live in such a way that brings glory to God through their marriage. The commitment to each other is extended to their children when they are born. In other words, the birth of a child should be a renewing of vows made with each other to love and to cherish "til death do us part."

The wedding ceremony of Adam and Eve was officiated by God. In Adam's wedding vows, the future of a marriage was prophesied. That a man would leave his father and mother and cleave to his wife. Further, Jesus said that what God has joined together, let no man put asunder.

The most common answer I get from unmarried couples regarding marriage is that it is just a piece of paper. They are referring to a marriage license, of course.

The marriage covenant is taken lightly these days, but with God it is very serious. God is a covenant-keeping God; when He makes a promise, He keeps it. His example of being a promise-keeping God should encourage us to keep our promises.

One of the covenants that God made was with Noah, right after the Flood. Soon after the Creation, man plunged into terrible sin. Man had no room in his heart for a relationship with God. God knew they would never turn to Him, and in His Sovereign will, the earth would be covered with a global flood to destroy all earthly life. The Bible says that Noah found grace in the eyes of the LORD.

In a world that was consumed with sin, Noah was the man who loved the LORD and worshiped Him, a righteous man, was given the task of building the Ark. God, demonstrating His patience and longsuffering, knew that the construction of the Ark would take 120 years. I would imagine that the news of Noah and his Ark spread all over the planet. Believe me, in Noah's pre-diluvium world, building an Ark in your front yard would be 'big news!'

When the Ark was finished, Noah and his family entered the ark as instructed by God. He then shut the door of the Ark and the rains came. When the flood waters receded, the Ark rested on Mt. Ararat in what is now modern Turkey. God then brought Noah and his family from the Ark. The first thing that Noah did was to build an altar and offer sacrifices to the LORD. God was very pleased and made a covenant with Noah.

"And I will establish my covenant with you,

neither shall all flesh be cut off any more by
the waters of a flood; neither shall there
anymore be a flood to destroy the earth.
And God said, this is the token of the
covenant which I make between me and you
and every living creature that is with you,
for perpetual generations. I do set my bow
in the cloud, and it shall be for a token of a
covenant between me and the earth. And it
shall come to pass, when I bring a cloud
over the earth, that the bow shall be seen in
the cloud: And I will remember my
covenant, which is between me and you and
every living creature of all flesh; and the
waters shall no more become a flood to
destroy all flesh. And the bow shall be in
the cloud; and I will look upon it, that I may
remember the everlasting covenant
between God and every living creature of all
flesh that is upon the earth. And God said
unto Noah, this is the token of the covenant,
which I have established between me and
all flesh that is upon the earth."
Genesis 9:11-17

So to this day, then we have a rainstorm and the sun comes out after the storm, we can see the rainbow. God is keeping the covenant with us that He made with Noah and to all generations to come.

The marriage license is signed by the witnesses at the wedding. They heard the promises made by the bride and groom. That promise is between the man and the woman and God. It is a sign of a covenant. It is not just a piece of paper.

ADDITIONAL SCRIPTURES:

"Therefore shall a man leave his father and his mother, and shall cleave unto his wife: and they shall be one flesh."
Genesis 2:24

"Whoso findeth a wife findeth a good thing, and obtaineth favour of the LORD."
Proverbs 18:22

"Husbands, love your wives, even as Christ also loved the church, and gave himself for it;"
Ephesians 5:25

"Be ye not unequally yoked together with unbelievers: for what fellowship hath righteousness with unrighteousness? and what communion hath light with darkness?"
II Corinthians 6:14

"Wherefore they are no more twain, but one flesh. What therefore God hath joined together, let not man put asunder."
Matthew 19:6

"Nevertheless let every one of you in particular so love his wife even as himself; and the wife see that she reverence her husband."
Ephesians 5:33

Notes:

24

The Praying Contest

One time when I was about eight years old, our family visited relatives in Illinois, and my dad was invited to preach at their small country church. I remember the building being medium-sized and full of people. During the service there was a time of prayer, and many of the men went to the altar to pray. They were all kneeling at the altar in a very humbling posture.

At first the praying was silent; then it wasn't long you could hear one of the men in a low mumble as he prayed. Then another man began to be heard, again in a low mumble. We couldn't tell what they were praying, but figured God would be listening anyway. Another man began to pray a little louder, then one of the other men elevated from a low mumble to a more normal voice. Not to be outdone, another man spoke in a normal voice too.

Even by the tender age of eight, I had heard a lot of praying, but I could tell this was mutating into something I had never witnessed before.

It was just a matter of seconds before one of the men raised his hand in prayer, then another man did the same thing. The second man raised his voice a bit louder than the first man. The third man raised his voice too with an occasional burst of volume for greater emphasis in his prayer. It was obvious the first man would not be outdone in his prayer, so he stood up!

They couldn't have been praying with their eyes closed in reverence, because a moment later they were all standing up. Now they had their hands raised, praying with a loud voice, moving around the altar in an ever emotional state. I think I was traumatized by the entire event!

God is not impressed with this type of expression. It does not matter if a man prays aloud or if he prays silently. God still hears his prayer.

When the Prophet Elijah challenged the prophets of the false god Baal, he said they would each build an altar, put a sacrifice on the altar, and the true God would answer with fire from heaven. Being the gentlemen that he was, he allowed them to go first. The scripture says,

> *"And they took the bullock which was given them, and they dressed it, and called on the name of Baal from morning even until noon, saying, O Baal, hear us. But there was no voice, nor any that answered. And they leaped upon the altar which was made. And it came to pass at noon, that Elijah mocked them, and said, cry aloud: for he is a god; either he is talking, or he is pursuing, or he is in a journey, or peradventure he sleepeth, and must be awaked. And they cried aloud, and cut themselves after their manner with knives and lancets, till the blood gushed out upon them. And it came to pass, when midday was past, and they prophesied until the time of the offering of the evening sacrifice, that there was neither voice, nor any to answer, nor any that*

regarded."
I Kings 18:26-29

The false prophets of Baal had a striking resemblance to the praying contest I attended as a young boy. I can just see these stately men dressed in their robes and adorned with the gold medallions of Baalism walking about, calling upon Baal to answer. The longer that Baal was silent, the more desperate their attempts to get the attention of their god.

I can't measure the sincerity of their prayer, but I do know that God responds to fervent prayer.

"The effectual fervent prayer of a righteous
man availeth much."
James 5:16b

Prayer is not a show. Even Jesus rebuked the heathen for their long prayers in public when He said,

"But when ye pray, use not vain repetitions,
as the heathen do: for they think that they
shall be heard for their much speaking. Be
not ye therefore like unto them: for your
Father knoweth what things ye have need
of, before ye ask him."
Matthew 6:7-8

And when thou prayest, thou shalt not be as
the hypocrites are: for they love to pray
standing in the synagogues and in the

corners of the streets, that they may be
seen of men. Verily I say unto you, they have
their reward. But thou, when thou prayest,
enter into thy closet, and when thou hast
shut thy door, pray to thy Father which is in
secret; and thy Father which seeth in secret
shall reward thee openly.
Matthew 6:5-6

So, prayer is not a contest. It is a time of intimate fellowship with our Heavenly Father. I encourage you to spend time with the Father in prayer. And if you can't think of anything to say, why not read to God from His own Holy Words, the Bible. The LORD God holds His Word above His name. Try Psalm 33, or perhaps Psalm 24.

"I will worship toward thy holy temple, and
praise thy name for thy lovingkindness and
for thy truth: for thou hast magnified thy
word above all thy name."
Psalm 138:2

The false prophets of Baal gave up, Elijah rebuilt his altar because the prophets of Baal had torn it down. He then placed the wood and the sacrifice on the altar as instructed by God. Next, Elijah had the sacrifice and the wood and the altar drenched with water. Elijah prayed a 63-word prayer acknowledging God, and he never once asked for fire.

"LORD God of Abraham, Isaac, and of Israel,
let it be known this day that thou art God in

*Israel, and that I am thy servant, and that I
have done all these things at thy word. Hear
me, O LORD, hear me, that this people may
know that thou art the LORD God, and that
thou hast turned their heart back again."*
I Kings 18:36-37

Simple, yet direct acknowledgement of the LORD is the living God. Then fire fell from heaven and consumed the sacrifice.

*"Then the fire of the LORD fell, and
consumed the burnt sacrifice, and the wood,
and the stones, and the dust, and licked up
the water that was in the trench. And when
all the people saw it, they fell on their faces:
and they said, The LORD, he is the God; the
LORD, he is the God.*
I Kings 18:38-39

It appears to me that the false prophets of Baal were out of a job!

ADDITIONAL SCRIPTURES:

*"If ye abide in me, and my words abide in
you, ye shall ask what ye will, and it shall be
done unto you."*
John 15:7

*"Therefore I say unto you, what things
soever ye desire, when ye pray, believe that
ye receive them, and ye shall have them."*

Mark 11:24

*"And I say unto you, Ask, and it shall be
given you; seek, and ye shall find; knock,
and it shall be opened unto you."*
Luke 11:9

*"Likewise the Spirit also helpeth our
infirmities: for we know not what we should
pray for as we ought: but the Spirit itself
maketh intercession for us with groanings
which cannot be uttered."*
Romans 8:26

*"Watch and pray, that ye enter not into
temptation: the spirit indeed is willing, but
the flesh is weak."*
Matthew 26:41

*"Call unto me, and I will answer thee, and
shew thee great and mighty things, which
thou knowest not."*
Jeremiah 33:3

Notes:

25

Ahem, Circumcision

The mind of man is carnal, meaning that he can take most any subject and twist its meaning away from what God intended for us. Let me say now that sex was created by God, and it is holy and pure within a marriage. Sex outside of a marriage is sin and breaks God's holy law. It might be the "in" thing to do in modern America, but it is still a sin against God.

When God called Abram out of the area of Ur (in modern day Iraq) and sent him to the Promised Land (modern day Israel) God made Abram a promise. The promise was that God would make Abram a great nation. He would have God's protection and guidance, and God promised Abram and his wife Sarai a son in their old age. As a covenant between God and Abram, several things happened. The promised son Isaac was to be Abram's by his wife Sarai, God then changed their name to Abraham and Sarah. God also commanded a sign of the covenant between God and Abraham that all human males in his house were to have their foreskins removed.

Abraham was a very rich man. He had men servants and maid servants who kept the flocks of sheep and tended the crops in the field. Abraham had camels, donkeys, and sheep; all required to sustain his household. When circumcision was first instituted, all males were circumcised, young and old alike. Abraham, his man servants, and other males living in his house.

Circumcision, a sign of the covenant, has been

ridiculed by man. Jokes are made in an attempt to make light of the covenant between God and Abraham. This is really a serious matter. There are many people who are not aware of the ancient significance of circumcision and its importance.

Obviously, for a spiritual man who has been circumcised, every day he lives he knows. Today, many baby boys are circumcised as a matter of health and hygiene. The Spiritually minded man is reminded daily of the ancient covenant with God that God will keep His promises. In His wisdom, God has made the covenant a private matter between the man and God. Think for a second, what the covenant would be for a man that say...had to put a notch in the lobe of his left ear. Then everyone would know; it would no longer be private.

Another aspect of, ahem, circumcision, is that the spiritually minded woman is also aware of the ancient covenant with God, that God keeps His promises. Each and every time the man and his wife come together in marriage, she also shares in the sign of the covenant with God.

One of the most dramatic narratives in the Scriptures about circumcision is the battle between David and the giant Goliath. When Goliath called for Israel to send their champion to fight, Goliath would swear and curse Israel by his false gods. When David heard it, he was incensed. David wanted to know the prize for killing Goliath, and then he asked the question "Who is this uncircumcised Philistine, that he would defy the armies of the living God?" The Philistines were the mortal enemies of God and Israel, and Goliath, this uncircumcised Philistine that was not in covenant, had to go.

David fought Goliath and defeated him with a shepherds sling and a stone. The final act is that David decapitated Goliath with his own sword.

Finally, The Apostle Paul made a brilliant illustration using circumcision. In his day, there were those who thought if someone was not circumcised that he was not saved in Christ. Paul said this in Galatians 5 and verse 6.

> *"For in Jesus Christ neither circumcision availeth anything, nor uncircumcision; but faith which worketh by love."*

So there is no profit in circumcision towards salvation. It is wrought by Jesus Christ' work on the cross of Calvary.

I close with this final thought from scripture,

> *"Neither is there salvation in any other: for there is none other name under heaven given among men, whereby we must be saved."*
> *Acts 4:12*

ADDITIONAL SCRIPTURES:

> *"For I know the thoughts that I think toward you, saith the LORD, thoughts of peace, and not of evil, to give you an expected end."*

Jeremiah 29:11

"Whereby are given unto us exceeding great and precious promises: that by these ye might be partakers of the divine nature, having escaped the corruption that is in the world through lust."
II Peter 1:4

"He hath remembered his covenant forever, the word which he commanded to a thousand generations. Which covenant he made with Abraham, and his oath unto Isaac; And confirmed the same unto Jacob for a law, and to Israel for an everlasting covenant:"
Psalm 105:8-10

"And because of all this we make a sure covenant, and write it; and our princes, Levites, and priests, seal unto it."
Nehemiah 9:38

"Behold, the days come, saith the LORD, that I will make a new covenant with the house of Israel, and with the house of Judah:"
Jeremiah 31:31

"For all the promises of God in him are yea, and in him Amen, unto the glory of God by us."
II Corinthians 1:20

Notes:

26

The Lady and the Lightning

For the last 30 years I have been associated with the electric utility industry. I have done a wide array of work, including building electric lines, maintenance, and service restoration. It is an honorable line of work as we provide energy to homes and businesses for their needs. Now that I have gotten older I have advanced into the support side of the business doing inventory management and other administrative duties. Honestly, there are some days where I would prefer to be outside with the crew working up a sweat.

One night years ago a line of storms moved through our service area, disrupting service to our customers. Winds usually cause trees to blow into the lines thus disrupting service, and then lightning will hit the lines causing equipment failure and other outages. All of these have to be addressed and corrected. We had worked all night changing damaged transformers and replacing blown line fuses. The sun came up and we were working on the last outage caused by a bad insulator on a pole.

The lineman was at the top of the pole changing the insulator when this lady walked out to our work area with a question. She had some chickens in a barn behind her house and was concerned about them. She then began our conversation:

"Do you work for the power company?" she asked.
"Yes" I said.

"Well, every time a storm blows through here our power goes out and my chickens don't like it. Can you do anything about that?"

"Yes Ma'am", I said, "we are changing an insulator that was damaged by lightning and your power will be back on in a few minutes."

"Can you do anything about that lightning?"

"We can do a lot of things Ma'am, but that lightning is between you and God!"

In reality, there is nothing we can do about where lightning will strike. God is in full control of all things, including the lightning. He has established physical laws and is He is true to them. When Job endured the loss of his family, business, and wealth, he became discouraged to the point that he asked to speak with God. At the time, I am sure Job had many things to say to God about the calamity in his life. He had lost his children, farms, and ranch; Job was a broken man with much grief. God did not allow Satan to take Job's life, but Job probably desired death for relief.

God then begin to speak to him in Job 38. God simply told Job to stand up and answer like a man. He then asked Job a series of questions; everything from what holds the earth in its orbit and how to deal with a fire breathing dragon.

In the end, Job put his hand over his mouth and said he abhorred himself, and indeed God is in control of everything.

I am encouraged when I hear again that God is in control. He is Sovereign over the weather, the stars, and even the heart of a king or a president.

There is much I cannot do, and I certainly can't control the lightning, but God can.

ADDITIONAL SCRIPTURES:

"And it came to pass on the third day in the morning, that there were thunders and lightnings, and a thick cloud upon the mount, and the voice of the trumpet exceeding loud; so that all the people that was in the camp trembled."
Exodus 19:16

"When he made a decree for the rain, and a way for the lightning of the thunder:"
Job 28:26

"Canst thou send lightnings, that they may go, and say unto thee, Here we are?"
Job 38:35

"He causeth the vapours to ascend from the ends of the earth; he maketh lightnings for the rain; he bringeth the wind out of his treasuries."
Psalm 135:7

"When he uttereth his voice, there is a multitude of waters in the heavens, and he causeth the vapours to ascend from the ends of the earth; he maketh lightnings with

rain, and bringeth forth the wind out of his treasures."
Jeremiah 10:13

"His countenance was like lightning, and his raiment white as snow:"
Matthew 28:3

Notes:

27

The Graciousness of Gratuity

It is social convention that when someone will dine in a real *live* restaurant, and not a fast hamburger place, then they are to show appreciation for the service by leaving gratuity, also known as a *tip*. Many full service restaurants only give their service personnel a token salary, so they live off their tips.

Jan and I will tip liberally, and not quibble over the amount. At a minimum, we will leave five dollars, and the more complicated the order, or the measure of service, we will respond accordingly. Sometimes we will go over the top a bit. You can tell by observing your server what is going on.

If your server is new, nerves will command the day as they service your table. A generous tip will show you observed their effort, even though everything did not work out as planned. Sometimes you can tell they are having problems, perhaps on the job or at home. Again, a generous tip really helps.

The Bible does not say anything about the words "tip" or "gratuity" in context of what we are discussing here. I believe Christian people should be known for their kindness and liberality when in a public place. What you do, or how you respond will have an influence on your outward testimony of Christ.

Service personnel know when a restaurant fills on a Sunday for lunch that most of these people have just left church. The way you act towards your waitress and how gracious you are with gratuity will speak volumes.

The waiter or waitress will appreciate your kindness and are very appreciative when you tip generously. It is not the waitress's fault the chef mixed up your order. To be honest what difference does it make? Put yourself in the place of the waitress. The place is packed, the kitchen is behind, and the best she can do is keep your glass full and replenish your chips and salsa. (Okay, I like Tex-Mex.)

We are Christian people in a public place being served by possible unbelievers. What an opportunity to demonstrate Christ. Take on the mind of Christ,

"And be not conformed to this world: but be
ye transformed by the renewing of your
mind, that ye may prove what is that good,
and acceptable, and perfect, will of God."
Romans 12:2

There is one final thing. When you go to a restaurant after church, don't preach to the waitress about not being in church herself. She was there at the restaurant early in the morning preparing for your arrival hours later. She could not be at church, for the restaurant is her only source of income. The demand of many Christian people coming to the restaurant after church required her to work; which is why she could not go to church in the first place.

In all things demonstrate Christ. When someone else is waiting on you and afterwards cleaning up your mess then become a generous tipper. And if for some reason the order is not correct, be kind. Still tip generously. It is a sad thing that Christian people will be so demanding in a public place and hold it against the server. If you feel the food or service is that bad, simply don't go back. In the meantime, remember that your actions can influence what others believe about Christ. Now, get out there and be generous.

ADDITIONAL SCRIPTURES:

"I have shewed you all things, how that so labouring ye ought to support the weak, and to remember the words of the Lord Jesus, how he said, It is more blessed to give than to receive."
Acts 20:35

"But whoso hath this world's good, and seeth his brother have need, and shutteth up his bowels [of compassion] from him, how dwelleth the love of God in him?"
I John 3:17

"He that hath pity upon the poor lendeth unto the LORD; and that which he hath given will he pay him again."
Proverbs 19:17

"Every man according as he purposeth in his heart, [so let him give]; not grudgingly, or of necessity: for God loveth a cheerful giver."

II Corinthians 9:7

"For where your treasure is, there will your heart be also."
Matthew 6:21

"Give, and it shall be given unto you; good measure, pressed down, and shaken together, and running over, shall men give into your bosom. For with the same measure that ye mete withal it shall be measured to you again."
Luke 6:38

Notes:

28

The Parking Kerfuffle

For a time, I worked in a corporate office as facilities manager; overseeing office maintenance and the occasional furniture purchase or office moves. I concluded one day that people who work in offices are selfish, never satisfied, and always wanting something done their way.

My boss came to me one day and told me the parking arrangements for the office had been changed by the owner of the building. It would be necessary for me to assign new parking spaces to the employees.

Now, I guess I am old fashioned. I believe if a person wants to park close to the front door they need to get to work early. Not so in the corporate world; there is a pecking order that's followed; each person watching out very selfishly for their own interest. As for me, I felt like I was trying to keep a room full of spoiled children happy.

I was given a new parking diagram then I asked Human Resources for a list of employees and their corporate title to be assigned a space. I began closest to the front door with the Executive Vice Presidents, then the Directors, Managers, and finally Supervisors. Each layer of management was pushed further out into the parking lot. I presented the final version to my Manager and he signed off on approval. The new parking assignments were then published.

It wasn't long that I received a scathing phone call

from a supervisor that was extremely unhappy because her parking assignment was one space further out than another supervisor who had a couple of months less service with the company.

Oops, I did not consider seniority when I made the assignments! My Manager also did not consider seniority when approving assignments. So now a lot of people are re-establishing the pecking order about where they park. It got so bad that the Director over our department reworked the parking assignments just to keep the peace.

I thought it strange because the Supervisor that started the whole kerfuffle about parking was a fitness enthusiast. Since a parking space is only eleven feet wide you would think that she would be thankful to be able to walk the extra eleven feet each day for fitness sake. But it wasn't the fitness, it was the prestige of having a couple of months' seniority on her peer; thus she wanted the closer parking space.

Seems a lot of people are working the pecking order these days, desiring the spotlight and the fame that goes with it. What's sad is that this attitude has also found its way in the Church, and is contrary to Jesus Christ.

The Apostle Paul encouraged us to be charitable or loving in our walk with Jesus Christ. Paul said in First Corinthians 13:4-7,

> *"Charity suffereth long, and is kind; charity envieth not; charity vaunteth not itself, is not puffed up, Doth not behave itself unseemly, seeketh not her own, is not easily provoked, thinketh no evil; Rejoiceth not in*

iniquity, but rejoiceth in the truth; Beareth all things, believeth all things, hopeth all things, endureth all things."

Those who are seeking position and control in the house of God are also contrary to the teaching of Jesus Christ. It is Jesus Christ that is the head of the church, the pastor is the shepherd of the sheep, seeking only their good for the glory of God.

Every once in a while, I will hear where a pastor is getting grief by the selfishness of someone in a church. Makes me wonder if folks ever read the Word of God for proper faith and church practice.

ADDITIONAL SCRIPTURES:

"For men shall be lovers of their own selves"
II Timothy 3:2

"For all seek their own, not the things which are Jesus Christ's."
Philippians 2:21

"From whence come wars and fightings among you? come they not hence, even of your lusts that war in your members?"
James 4:1

"Through desire a man, having separated himself, seeketh and intermeddleth with all wisdom."

Proverbs 18:1

"Blessed is the man that walketh not in the counsel of the ungodly, nor standeth in the way of sinners, nor sitteth in the seat of the scornful. But his delight is in the law of the LORD; and in his law doth he meditate day and night."
Psalm 1:1-2

"Let your light so shine before men, that they may see your good works, and glorify your Father which is in heaven."
Matthew 5:16

Notes:

29

The Heart of the King

I have always been fascinated with the Biblical narrative of the Kings of Israel. The lives of these men are given to us as examples of how to live. They teach is the rewards for obedience to God's commandments and the punishment for disobedience. The LORD God is Sovereign of all, and is in full control. This also includes presidents, kings, and other national leaders.

There are many pieces to this puzzle. The first is when God said that we can learn from the animals. Let's observe the following,

"But ask now the beasts, and they shall teach thee; and the fowls of the air, and they shall tell thee: Or speak to the earth, and it shall teach thee: and the fishes of the sea shall declare unto thee. Who knoweth not in all these that the hand of the LORD hath wrought this?
Job 12:7-9

If we can learn from the beasts, we can learn from the Kings.

There are those who will compare different presidents to each other, as well as other world leaders. In Scripture, it mainly refers to the Kings, but an application of principles can be made to presidents and other leaders.

Before Israel had a King, Israel was ruled by Theocracy, or by God's rule. God would give commandments to the priest and they, in turn, would instruct the people. Further, God gave the law to Moses, which was subsequently given to the Children of Israel.

Now when God gave the law to Moses, God inserted instructions for the King. It's a lengthy passage but please read it carefully.

"When thou art come unto the land which the LORD thy God giveth thee, and shalt possess it, and shalt dwell therein, and shalt say, I will set a king over me, like as all the nations that are about me; Thou shalt in any wise set him king over thee, whom the LORD thy God shall choose: one from among thy brethren shalt thou set king over thee: thou mayest not set a stranger over thee, which is not thy brother. But he shall not multiply horses to himself, nor cause the people to return to Egypt, to the end that he should multiply horses: forasmuch as the LORD hath said unto you, Ye shall henceforth return no more that way. Neither shall he multiply wives to himself, that his heart turn not away: neither shall he greatly multiply to himself silver and gold. And it shall be, when he sitteth upon the throne of his kingdom, that he shall write him a copy of this law in a book out of that which is before the priests the Levites:

*And it shall be with him, and he shall read
therein all the days of his life: that he may
learn to fear the LORD his God, to keep all
the words of this law and these statutes, to
do them: That his heart be not lifted up
above his brethren, and that he turn not
aside from the commandment, to the right
hand, or to the left: to the end that he may
prolong his days in his kingdom, he, and his
children, in the midst of Israel."
Deuteronomy 17:14-20*

I am not aware of any king that obeyed this law. At least I can't find it in scripture. Even King David, the apple of God's eye, had several wives. It was his large family that gave him much sorrow at the end of his reign.

Another item is that Kings were not to accumulate wealth. The Bible mentions they are not to multiply horses, meaning wealth. Every decision made was to be for the good of the people and according to God's Law.

The Bible also says this about the heart of a King:

*"The king's heart is in the hand of the LORD,
as the rivers of water:
he turneth it whithersoever he will."
Proverbs 21:1*

God is absolutely sovereign, and when it seems to us that a leader is doing something unbelievably crazy, God is still in control.

We should really be comforted by the fact that God

is in control. I hear that a lot and I wonder if people really know what that means.

> *"For my thoughts are not your thoughts, neither are your ways my ways, saith the LORD. For as the heavens are higher than the earth, so are my ways higher than your ways, and my thoughts than your thoughts."*
> Isaiah 55:8-9

The takeaway from this verse is even if we do not understand what is going on, God does. Many times I hear where people desire a different leader, or that the leader would do something different. Many do not understand why a leader would do the things he does, but God has his heart. By heart, we mean the being of the man or woman. Their spirit, as it were.

There is a lesson here for us from the animals that might help make sense of all this. This lesson is about the eagle and the ostrich. Both are birds, each have their own charms, but let's see what God says of them.

> *"Gavest thou the goodly wings unto the peacocks? or wings and feathers unto the ostrich? Which leaveth her eggs in the earth, and warmeth them in dust, And forgetteth that the foot may crush them, or that the wild beast may break them. She is hardened against her young ones, as though they were not hers: her labour is in*

vain without fear; Because God hath
deprived her of wisdom, neither hath he
imparted to her understanding. What time
she lifteth up herself on high, she scorneth
the horse and his rider."
Job 39:13-18

The key point here is the Ostrich has no concern for her young because God has not given her wisdom. She does not understand her eggs could be crushed in the sand. However, she can run. Probably outrunning a trained horse and rider.

By contrast, God spoke these words about the eagle.

"Doth the eagle mount up at thy command,
and make her nest on high? She dwelleth
and abideth on the rock, upon the crag of
the rock, and the strong place. From thence
she seeketh the prey, and her eyes behold
afar off."
Job 39:27-29

Now we have an example of an animal which exercises wisdom, building her nest where her young will be safe. She can see her prey at a distance with her keen eyesight. I have heard that an eagle can see a fish in a pond from two miles away.

Just as God has not given an ostrich wisdom, so has God moved in the heart of a King. Consider this example,

"And the LORD said unto Moses, When thou goest to return into Egypt, see that thou do all those wonders before Pharaoh, which I have put in thine hand: but I will harden his heart, that he shall not let the people go."
Exodus 4:21

Here we see that God has moved in the heart of the King of Egypt, the Pharaoh. God moved in his heart every time there was a respite from the plagues, and He changed his mind. That was of the LORD. There were ten plagues, and ten times God hardened Pharaoh's heart.

Further, God hardened Pharaoh's heart one last time, when he decided to chase after the Hebrews. To me it is insane that after enduring all the plagues and the death of his son that the Pharaoh would do such a thing as chase after the Hebrews. God had clearly demonstrated His sovereignty through judgements upon Egypt. The Pharaoh was just a man, but he challenged the LORD God, the Creator. If God can withhold wisdom from an Ostrich, He can also withhold wisdom from the heart of a king. This is done for the glory of God. We might not understand it, but it is so.

The Hebrews were God's chosen people and they originally went to Egypt to escape a famine in the land of Canaan. There, they multiplied and grew. The Egyptians, afraid that the Hebrews might turn on them if given an opportunity, enslaved them. Further, as the Hebrews grew in number, the Pharaoh ordered the killing of all the newborn Hebrew males. In the last plague, God killed all the firstborn of Egypt. Vengeance is mine sayeth the

LORD.

Look carefully at the power of God as Pharaoh chases the Hebrews.

> *"And I will harden Pharaoh's heart, that he shall follow after them; and I will be honoured upon Pharaoh, and upon all his host; that the Egyptians may know that I am the LORD. And they did so. And it was told the king of Egypt that the people fled: and the heart of Pharaoh and of his servants was turned against the people, and they said, Why have we done this, that we have let Israel go from serving us?"*
> *Exodus 14:4-5*

Notice that Pharaoh's servants also have a hardened heart. As they chase after the Hebrews, which are stopped at the Red Sea, God protected them with a cloud of darkness to the Egyptians, but light to the Hebrews. God then opened up the Red Sea so the Hebrews could cross over. Do you agree with me that Pharaoh is doing something absolutely crazy to chase after the Hebrews? But, notice this verse:

> *"And I, behold, I will harden the hearts of the Egyptians, and they shall follow them: and I will get me honour upon Pharaoh, and upon all his host, upon his chariots, and upon his horsemen. And the Egyptians shall know that I am the LORD, when I have*

gotten me honour upon Pharaoh, upon his
chariots, and upon his horsemen."
Exodus 14:17-18

God will always be glorified. The Hebrew are His chosen people, and He will be glorified in them.

After Israel had crossed the Red Sea, The King of Egypt had his army pursue Israel. Then the unthinkable happened.

"And Moses stretched forth his hand over
the sea, and the sea returned to his strength
when the morning appeared; and the
Egyptians fled against it; and the LORD
overthrew the Egyptians in the midst of the
sea. And the waters returned, and covered
the chariots, and the horsemen, and all the
host of Pharaoh that came into the sea after
them; there remained not so much as one of
them."
Exodus 14:27-28

Finally, God not only holds the heart of the King, He puts them in power.

"Daniel answered and said, Blessed be the
name of God for ever and ever: for wisdom
and might are his: And he changeth the
times and the seasons: he removeth kings,
and setteth up kings: he giveth wisdom unto
the wise, and knowledge to them that know

understanding:"
Daniel 2:20-21

God is in full control including the heart of the King. He will take care of any wrong done by them. Further, it is not for us to worry about the "King", but rather on praising God.

Have you ever prayed for a different "King"? Since God has that under control, perhaps our prayer time would be better spent praising His name and praying for revival.

And don't worry, revival can come, no matter who we have for a King.

ADDITIONAL SCRIPTURES:

"Let every soul be subject unto the higher powers. For there is no power but of God: the powers that be are ordained of God."
Romans 13:1

"The king's heart is in the hand of the LORD, as the rivers of water: he turneth it whithersoever he will."
Proverbs 21:1

"For the kingdom is the LORD'S: and he is the governor among the nations."
Psalm 22:28

"That they may know from the rising of the

sun, and from the west, that there is none beside me. I am the LORD, and there is none else."
Isaiah 45:6

"And the LORD said unto him, Go, return on thy way to the wilderness of Damascus: and when thou comest, anoint Hazael to be king over Syria:"
I Kings 19:15

"See, I have this day set thee over the nations and over the kingdoms, to root out, and to pull down, and to destroy, and to throw down, to build, and to plant."
Jeremiah 1:10

Notes:

30

The Eleventh Commandment

While growing up as a teenager I would attend a summer camp at Lake Texoma with activities centered on the Bible. I actually enjoyed camp time. The weather was nice, the food was good, and girls were everywhere.

One year there was a guy at camp who became a celebrity of sorts. He had a following of several teens and we would see him walking around the campus with his disciples in tow. A time or two he would sit on a small hill in the shade of the mess hall and would give a talk. I observed this from afar while waiting in line for dinner.

One afternoon the word spread all over camp that this guy had said there were eleven commandments. Eleven? Naturally my curiosity was eager to find out this new revelation. As it turned out, the supposed eleventh commandment was "Thou shalt not pollute." Actually, it made me feel bad about pouring used motor oil around the garage to kill the weeds. However, the guy denied he prophesied the eleventh commandment but the damage was done. I learned that people will believe anything.

The Ten Commandments as given in Exodus chapter 20 are the guide for religious and moral duties of man. For centuries these commandments have been found posted in the home, church, and many government or public buildings. The Ten Commandments give men purpose and direction as he lives his life. Sadly, the commandments are under a growing attack to have them removed from public view. I believe this movement to remove the Ten Commandments from our lives is an attack direct from the devil himself. The devil knows when once the Ten Commandments are removed from our lives that we will move deeper into depravity and farther away from God.

I recommend every home display the Ten Commandments for all to see. We need to teach them to our children. We, as adults, need to embrace them. We need to practice them in our lives. If we don't do this, we will begin to believe anything.

For the record, here are the Ten Commandments.

1. *"I am the LORD thy God, thou shalt have no other gods before me."*

2. *"You shall not have any false idols."*

3. *"You shall not take the name of the LORD thy God in vain."*

4. *"Remember the Sabbath to keep it holy."*

5. *"Honor thy father and thy mother."*

6. *"Thou shalt not kill."*

7. *"Thou shalt not commit adultery."*

8. *"Thou shalt not steal."*

9. *"Thou shalt not bear false witness against thy neighbor."*

10. *"Thou shalt not covet."*

May God bless you.

ADDITIONAL SCRIPTURES:

"Ye shall not add unto the word which I command you, neither shall ye diminish ought from it, that ye may keep the commandments of the LORD your God which I command you."
Deuteronomy 4:2

"What thing soever I command you, observe to do it: thou shalt not add thereto, nor diminish from it."
Deuteronomy 12:32

"But he answered and said, Every plant, which my heavenly Father hath not planted, shall be rooted up."
Matthew 15:13

"Add thou not unto his words, lest he reprove thee, and thou be found a liar."
Proverbs 30:6

"I marvel that ye are so soon removed from him that called you into the grace of Christ unto another gospel: Which is not another; but there be some that trouble you, and would pervert the gospel of Christ. But though we, or an angel from heaven, preach any other gospel unto you than that which we have preached unto you, let him be

accursed."
Galatians 1:6-8

"All scripture is given by inspiration of God, and is profitable for doctrine, for reproof, for correction, for instruction in righteousness: That the man of God may be perfect, thoroughly furnished unto all good works."
II Timothy 3:16-17

"The words of the LORD are pure words: as silver tried in a furnace of earth, purified seven times."
Psalm 12:6

Notes:

31

The Upside of Going Uphill

My doctor draw blood periodically to determine the state of my health. For example, several years now I have dealt with elevated blood sugar levels. The doctor has told me to diet and exercise, and for the exercise portion of my health program I ride a bicycle around the neighborhood in Roxton.

For the record, it has been a very long time since I rode a bicycle. Balancing is not a problem, but my legs are not used to the rigors of pedaling more than a couple of miles. However, within that couple of miles, I will raise my heart rate and breathing, so it must be doing some good.

A few months ago my son decided to do a bike ride in Dallas on the Trinity River levees. He also decided to take me along. It was an organized event where we had to pay a few dollars to participate. They gave us a t-shirt at the end of the ride, so it was good. The ride was divided into two sections, a six-mile ride and a sixty-mile ride. I knew I couldn't do a sixty-mile ride, but I agreed to the six-mile route.

The ride was mostly on flat ground and partly paved roadways, so I was determined to finish the ride. My son had no problem as he is an avid rider, but for me things begin to wear thin around the third mile. I had to stop a couple of times to catch my breath and get a drink of water.

We finally finished the six miles, but there was not

any glory. The last 200 feet of the ride was uphill on the side of a levee of the Trinity River. It was a real steep grade and I was simply exhausted. My legs felt like wet noodles; no strength left in them. My son knew I was at the end of my limit so we decided to push our bikes up the hill. Even as we dismounted our bikes and pushed the last 200 feet, there were folks on each side of the trail clapping and encouraging us as we finished the ride.

I have heard it said that a tree will not develop strong roots if it never endures a storm. Likewise, it is the difficulty of exercise which works our muscles to make them stronger.

The upside of going uphill is simply this, it makes us stronger. Sometimes we will endure a financial hardship. Going up that hill we learn the lessons of what got us there in the first place and we become financially wiser and stronger. Sometimes we endure health issues. Again, going up that hill will make us stronger and more courageous so we can later comfort someone else as they endure sickness.

The Apostle Paul encourages us with these words,

"And not only so, but we glory in
tribulations also: knowing that tribulation
worketh patience; And patience,
experience; and experience, hope:"
Romans 5:3-4

Just as I have to make bike riding a challenge by taking on a hill, Christians must endure as different challenges come into our lives. The Bible says that God will not test us more than we can endure.

> *"There hath no temptation taken you but such as is common to man: but God is faithful, who will not suffer you to be tempted above that ye are able; but will with the temptation also make a way to escape, that ye may be able to bear it."*
> *I Corinthians 10:13*

Mountains are nothing more than big hills. Jesus said that if we had faith as of a grain of mustard seed we could command and move a mountain.

> *"And Jesus said unto them, Because of your unbelief: for verily I say unto you, If ye have faith as a grain of mustard seed, ye shall say unto this mountain, Remove hence to yonder place; and it shall remove; and nothing shall be impossible unto you."*
> *Matthew 17:20*

I have not heard of any mountains moving recently; there must not be much faith going on. A few years ago I enjoyed a worship service with a black congregation and their preacher was encouraging folks about dealing with mountains. He said that sometimes we go over the mountain, and sometimes we go around the mountain. We do as the Lord and Master directs us. And sometimes, we go through the mountain. And no matter how we deal with that mountain, we give the LORD God the Glory and

Praise for it.

ADDITIONAL SCRIPTURES:

"Now unto him that is able to do exceeding abundantly above all that we ask or think, according to the power that worketh in us,"
Ephesians 3:20

"And though I have the gift of prophecy, and understand all mysteries, and all knowledge; and though I have all faith, so that I could remove mountains, and have not charity, I am nothing."
I Corinthians 13:2

"And Jesus answering saith unto them, Have faith in God. For verily I say unto you, That whosoever shall say unto this mountain, Be thou removed, and be thou cast into the sea; and shall not doubt in his heart, but shall believe that those things which he saith shall come to pass; he shall have whatsoever he saith."
Mark 11:22-23

"Verily, verily, I say unto you, He that believeth on me, the works that I do shall he do also; and greater works than these shall he do; because I go unto my Father."
John 14:12

"Now Moses kept the flock of Jethro his father in law, the priest of Midian: and he led the flock to the backside of the desert, and came to the mountain of God, even to Horeb."
Exodus 3:1

"Now therefore give me this mountain, whereof the LORD spake in that day; for thou heardest in that day how the Anakims were there, and that the cities were great and fenced: if so be the LORD will be with me, then I shall be able to drive them out, as the LORD said."
Joshua 14:12

Notes:

32

Johnny Lidster's Nail

The electric company I work for has safety meetings every week. We also have a short meeting at the jobsite called a *Tailboard*. The purpose of the Tailboard is to identify all the hazards of the job site to prevent an accident or injury.

Back in the mid 1960's when the church in Grapevine underwent construction we did not have safety meetings, but hazards were everywhere. One common hazard on a building job site is a nail protruding skyward out of board on the ground. One wrong step and a person could get a nail in the foot.

Johnny Lidster was a member of the church, and he was also a contractor. My dad hired him to take care of the third addition to the church.

I remember Johnny Lidster's gray-and-white striped overalls. Seems every pocket on his overalls was put to good use with a tape measure, pencil, pliers, and a chalk string. There was even a loop where his hammer was handy for the next task.

The work was progressing and some folks had gathered around to admire what had been done. I am sure that Mr. Lidster was experienced enough to watch for the hazards on the job site. Seconds later he groaned a bit, and he immediately lifted his foot off the ground. Distracted, Johnny Lidster had stepped on a nail. With the weight of his leg bearing down, the nail easily protruded the sole of his shoes, went through his sock, and pierced into his foot.

When Mr. Lidster groaned he lifted his foot to see the small board there with a nail piercing the sole of his shoe and foot. I was standing nearby and could tell it was in pretty deep. Then that sick, nervous, nauseous feeling came over me. Johnny Lidster reached down and with a tug pulled the nail out of his foot. I got a sicklier weak feeling in my stomach as he pulled it out. The men standing around helped Mr. Lidster sit down and he removed his shoe. Yes, the presence of a little blood confirmed the damage, and off they went to the local clinic for a tetanus shot.

We as Christians should be amazed at what Jesus Christ did for us on the cross of Calvary. The torture which Jesus endured before His crucifixion was horrendous. The Roman soldiers were expert at inflicting unimaginable pain on their victims, and after the loss of a lot of blood they required Jesus to carry His cross to Calvary where He would be crucified. Jesus collapsed under the weight of the cross, so a man named Simon was compelled to carry the cross for Him.

The nails used in the crucifixion were very large, more on the order of an iron spike, it makes a 16 penny nail look pale in comparison. The ordeal of the crucifixion was done in such a way the human body would endure intense pain, as if every nerve is exposed and the brain registers nothing but extreme pain.

"But he was wounded for our
transgressions, he was bruised for our
iniquities: the chastisement of our peace

was upon him; and with his stripes we are
healed."
Isaiah 53:5

We go to church in our new cars, dressed in nice clothes, and sit in judgement of the service while the air conditioning keeps us cool; yet we never become convicted of our sin for which Jesus Christ gave His life. *"I didn't like the sermon. I don't like that song. The air conditioning is too cool. The preacher kept us 5 minutes after 12. I don't care what the preacher says, I am not coming back tonight. Mrs. Doodlewack offended me and I am never going back to that church. I don't care what the Bible says, I am not giving any more money to missions."* And the list goes on.

Yet in all this, Jesus Christ loves you anyway, and gave His life on the cross as the Supreme sacrifice for your sin. There is nothing you can do before God that will cover your sin, except the atoning work of Jesus Christ.

Johnny Lidster later returned to his work. The extension to the front of the building was finished, and we could accommodate more people at services to worship our LORD God.

ADDITIONAL SCRIPTURES:

"Surely he hath borne our griefs, and carried our
sorrows: yet we did esteem him stricken, smitten
of God, and afflicted."
Isaiah 53:4

"But he was wounded for our transgressions, he
was bruised for our iniquities: the chastisement
of our peace was upon him; and with his stripes

we are healed."
Isaiah 53:5

"I gave my back to the smiters, and my cheeks to them that plucked off the hair: I hid not my face from shame and spitting."
Isaiah 50:6

"But Jeshurun waxed fat, and kicked: thou art waxen fat, thou art grown thick, thou art covered with fatness; then he forsook God which made him, and lightly esteemed the Rock of his salvation."
Deuteronomy 32:15

"Looking unto Jesus the author and finisher of our faith; who for the joy that was set before him endured the cross, despising the shame, and is set down at the right hand of the throne of God."
Hebrews 12:2

"And shall deliver him to the Gentiles to mock, and to scourge, and to crucify him: and the third day he shall rise again."
Matthew 20:19

Notes:

33

A Matter of Faith

I enjoy the sciences, space travel, and astronomy. During the early 1960's, NASA had accepted a challenge from President John F. Kennedy to put a man on the moon and return him safely before the end of the decade. Thereafter, it seemed that every few months another rocket was launched with a manned capsule to conduct more experiments in preparation for the journey to the Moon.

One day when I was about 14 years old I wrote a letter to NASA asking for information on the U.S. rocket fleet. It wasn't long until NASA sent me posters about rockets and their specifications. I learned the names of all the engines, their thrust ratings, the fuel the rocket carried, and payload.

The sciences have discovered many things: how to increase the yield of a crop, or new technologies that can improve quality of life. Scientists have also looked through their telescopes at the universe to postulate theories of our origins. Their arguments are very convincing at times. One must remember that these arguments and theories appeal to the carnal nature of man. Since man is not predisposed to believe in God then the arguments of origins and the universe can make sense.

So one might wonder why a person that likes science so much can believe the Bible and the narrative about God and His creation that was written thousands of years ago.

I sometimes refer to this as the Holmes Law of Opposites. It seems most everything between science and the Bible are opposite of each other.

For example, science tells us that the universe is 13.7 billion years old while the narrative of the Bible says the universe is about 6 thousand years old! According to the Bible the heavens and earth were created first, then the stars. Science says the universe and stars came to be, then the earth.

Science also says that at the time the earth was formed it was covered with lava and fire. The Bible says the earth was covered with water. Finally, science tells us that the dinosaurs lived on the earth for over 135 million years and died out when an asteroid hit the earth over 65 million years ago. But, the Bible says that God created all animal life on the earth on the fifth and sixth days of creation. Science uses carbon 14 dating methods to extrapolate their dates and timetables. To be frank, it can be very convincing, but I do not believe their arguments.

God created a stone six thousand years ago and carbon 14 tests today make it to be millions of years old. Why is that? Because God created all things with the appearance of great age. On the fourth day when God created the fruit bearing trees they were mature bearing fruit. On the fifth day of creation birds were mature and flying, sea creatures were fully grown, filling the oceans.

For me, it is a matter of faith. The writer of Hebrews in chapter 11 and verse 3 said,

"Through faith we understand that the

*worlds were framed by the word of God, so
that things which are seen were not made
of things which do appear."*

I believe by faith God spoke the command for creation and all which we see in the universe was instantly created from nothing!

The Bible tells us in Isaiah chapter 57 and verse 15 that God inhabits eternity. Since God dwelt in the dimension of eternity then time and outer space did not exist until God spoke it into existence. In Genesis chapter 1 and verse 1 it says,

*"In the beginning God created the heaven
and the earth."*

God created the dimension of time so that there could be a beginning, God created the heaven to have a place in time for the universe. After the heaven was created then God created the earth as a planet entirely covered with water.

The creation narrative brings a lot to those who believe in God. The Bible tells us that God is all powerful, and that God is not limited in any way, including His incredible creative ability to make a stone six thousand years old appear to be millions of years old.

ADDITIONAL SCRIPTURES:

*"And God saw everything that he had made,
and, behold, it was very good. And the evening
and the morning were the sixth day."*

Genesis 1:31

"I have made the earth, and created man upon it: I, even my hands, have stretched out the heavens, and all their host have I commanded."
Isaiah 45:12

"For by him were all things created, that are in heaven, and that are in earth, visible and invisible, whether they be thrones, or dominions, or principalities, or powers: all things were created by him, and for him:"
Colossians 1:16

"All things were made by him; and without him was not anything made that was made."
John 1:3

"I beheld the earth, and, lo, it was without form, and void; and the heavens, and they had no light."
Jeremiah 4:23

"Thou, even thou, art LORD alone; thou hast made heaven, the heaven of heavens, with all their host, the earth, and all things that are therein, the seas, and all that is therein, and thou preservest them all; and the host of heaven worshippeth thee."
Nehemiah 9:6

Notes:

34

Eat Your Vegetables!

When I was a youngster at home we generally ate staple groceries; beans, potatoes, and the occasional chicken. Mom knew we needed variety in our diet and would encourage more plants, so she would encourage us to eat eggplant, squash, and other varieties like that. To this day I do not understand the eggplant or the squash.

Now I really like a home grown, vine-ripe tomato. I will also eat cucumbers and iceberg lettuce.

When God created life on the earth He provided a diet of plants for us to enjoy. The instruction was for all life, so all animals and man would adhere to the Word of God.

> *"And God said, Behold, I have given you*
> *every herb bearing seed, which is upon the*
> *face of all the earth, and every tree, in the*
> *which is the fruit of a tree yielding seed; to*
> *you it shall be for meat. And to every beast*
> *of the earth, and to every fowl of the air,*
> *and to everything that creepeth upon the*
> *earth, wherein there is life, I have given*
> *every green herb for meat: and it was so."*
> Genesis 1:29-30

These words change how most people perceive the animal kingdom. We know that many beasts are predators, and some are the prey. But the instruction to eat plants was before the fall of man. It was before sin.

In Genesis 3 we read where the devil, disguised as a serpent, approached Eve to tempt her. She yielded to the serpent, and likewise gave Adam the fruit that was forbidden. Their sin was not the fruit itself, but disobedience to the Creator God. In the persons of Adam and Eve the LORD God no longer was given first place, but their own will.

As a result of their sin, the man would work all his days by the sweat of his brow and the earth would no longer be easy to farm. The woman would bear children in sorrow, and the serpent was doomed to crawl on his belly in the dust. The earth would bring forth thorns and stickers, and death would be known. Now we have the rise of the predator and the lowing of the prey. Predators included the big cats, wolves, some reptiles, and some dinosaurs, and more.

It is hard to imagine something like a Tyrannosaurus-Rex eating plants. That is totally contrary to what we are told by the Hollywood movie makers. After all, the T-Rex has such a big gaping mouth and shark-like teeth it would seem impossible that he would eat plants. I believe the Word of God to be true so I have no problem believing a T-Rex would eat plants. So did the lion and the wolves.

I am not a nutritional expert, but I have heard the best foods are just inside the grocery store, the produce section, and along the outside walls. The foods on the inner aisles of the store are generally processed finely with many additives and preservatives. The closer your foods get to the Garden of Eden the better they will be.

ADDITIONAL SCRIPTURES:

"Prove thy servants, I beseech thee, ten days; and let them give us pulse to eat, and water to drink."
Daniel 1:12

"Every moving thing that liveth shall be meat for you; even as the green herb have I given you all things. But flesh with the life thereof, which is the blood thereof, shall ye not eat."
Genesis 9:3-4

"For one believeth that he may eat all things: another, who is weak, eateth herbs."
Romans 14:2

"Be not among winebibbers; among riotous eaters of flesh: For the drunkard and the glutton shall come to poverty: and drowsiness shall clothe a man with rags."
Proverbs 23:20-21

"Whether therefore ye eat, or drink, or whatsoever ye do, do all to the glory of God."
I Corinthians 10:31

"Better is a dinner of herbs where love is,

than a stalled ox and hatred therewith."
Proverbs 15:17

Notes:

35

A Silver Moon on a Sunny Day

When I was about nine years old our Sunday school class of young boys went on a raccoon hunt. I had never been hunting before so I had no idea what to expect. However, most of the other boys had been hunting for raccoon before and they were very confident about the night ahead. All I was told is that I would need a flashlight.

Interesting thing about the flashlight; at the time it was believed you could put a dead or near dead battery in the refrigerator for a while and it would recharge. Dad let me borrow his flashlight, and I dug up every old battery I could find and placed them in the refrigerator so I would be prepared for a full night.

When the hunt started, the boys were talking loud and rough-housing about, but it was hard to hear all the commotion above the bark and howling of the dogs. It seemed we walked for miles trying to keep up with the group, and I had Dad's flashlight and a coat pocket full of cold batteries.

Someone came up to me and said I could turn the flash light off because of the moonlight. I did, and could not believe how bright the moon lit the earth. I put the flashlight away, and navigated by the light of the moon. They say we treed a raccoon that night, but, I do not recall seeing it, much less what happened to it.

It was the fourth day of creation when God made the sun, moon, and the stars. The Biblical narrative is opposite of what the scientific community will tell us.

They said the universe with all the stars were formed first, and then the earth. But the eye witness account we have from God is exactly the opposite. The earth was created first, and then God made the Sun to be a greater light in the daytime, and the moon to give a light reflected from the sun to the earth at night.

The phases of the moon give us a different perspective of moonlight about every seven days, the most glorious is the full moon on a clear winters evening. The light reflected to the earth is just stunning, enough to give someone the urge to go hunting.

Sometimes, when the moon is right and the sun is right we can see the moon in the sky on a bright sunny day. When that happens, one cannot tell that the moon is making a difference to the light cast on the earth, but the view is remarkable.

"And God made two great lights; the greater light to rule the day, and the lesser light to rule the night: he made the stars also."
Genesis 1:16

"The heavens declare the glory of God; and the firmament sheweth his handywork."
Psalm 19:1

What's even more remarkable (to me at least) is you do not see the sun at night shining with the moon. Just a thought.

The scriptures have much to say about the moon

and the sun in the end times, about them being darkened and even the moon will turn to blood. Our Sovereign God will not have a problem doing that in His Divine will.

The moon is actually in the daytime sky quite often, but we cannot see it. Same thing for the stars. They are always there, but we cannot see them during the day. However, I have read where some real savvy amateur astronomers with powerful equipment can see some stars and a couple of planets in the daytime.

Our Creator God is incredible for His thoughtfulness towards us, even to give us a fantastic show in the heavens from time to time. I do not take it lightly about seeing the moon on a bright sunny day. The Holy One is demonstrating His omnipotence once again.

ADDITIONAL SCRIPTURES:

"When I consider thy heavens, the work of thy fingers, the moon and the stars, which thou hast ordained;"
Psalm 8:3

"He appointed the moon for seasons: the sun knoweth his going down."
Psalm 104:19

"Praise ye him, sun and moon: praise him, all ye stars of light."
Psalm 148:3

"And it shall come to pass, that from one

new moon to another, and from one
sabbath to another, shall all flesh come to
worship before me, saith the LORD."
Isaiah 66:23

"Thus saith the LORD, which giveth the sun
for a light by day, and the ordinances of the
moon and of the stars for a light by night,
which divideth the sea when the waves
thereof roar; The LORD of hosts is his
name:"
Jeremiah 31:35

"And the city had no need of the sun,
neither of the moon, to shine in it: for the
glory of God did lighten it, and the Lamb is
the light thereof."
Revelation 21:23

Notes:

36

Drawing a Line in the Sand

There are times when a decision must be made. Most everyone has heard about the line in the sand. The saying goes back a long way, but is most commonly associated with the defense of the Alamo in San Antonio, Texas.

Mexican General Santa Anna had sent Lt. Colonel Travis a letter stating that if they did not surrender, everyone in the Alamo compound would be killed. Lt. Colonel Travis, committed to stay and fight, pulled his sword and drew a line in the sand. He then asked for those who would cross the line and fight with him, which would mean certain death. All but one in the Alamo crossed the line. The cause was that important. At stake was freedom and liberty.

One does not have to see a literal line in the sand to make a decision. It was Moses who was on the mount receiving the Law from God and when he came down from the mount he found where the people had abandoned God and began worshiping idols. Further, in all the revelry, Aaron the priest had made the Children of Israel shed their clothes to their shame. Moses was enraged. Moses then, in his anger, cast the tables of stone to the ground breaking them.

He then drew the imaginary "line in the sand," as it were, and asked, "Who is on the LORD'S side?" The tribe of Levi crossed the line and Moses commanded that those who worshipped the idols were to be killed.

This may seem harsh, but we must remember in God's holy law we are to worship Him only. The LORD God is very, very, holy, and we must never forget His holiness. Further, we are not to worship any other gods for the LORD God is the Living God. He is the Sovereign of all things in eternity and on the earth. He is the God of Abraham, Isaac, and Jacob. He is the LORD God of Creation. It is He that made the heavens and the earth, and all that in them is.

"The earth is the LORD's, and the fulness thereof; the world, and they that dwell therein."
Psalm 24:1

It is now time for many of us to decide whether or not to cross that line; to make the decision to serve the LORD and Creator.

What is it that holds you back? Are you afraid that you will be alone? Are you afraid of your friends or family? Are you worried about what others might say or think?

I choose to serve the LORD. I will be on His side in the battle. I know that the LORD will be victorious, of which I have no doubt. I choose to be on His side when the arguments arise about creation or global warming. I choose to be on His side when we talk about the virgin birth of Jesus Christ. I choose to be on His side when the doubters scoff at the resurrection of Jesus Christ. I choose to be on His side when He judges this earth in the end times.

I choose to honor and love Him. I choose to attend worship services when His people gather to sing praises to His name and the Word of God is explained in the preaching.

I choose to read the Word of God, the Bible. I choose to pray. I choose to open my mind to His leading and to His will. I trust Him for He is in control of all things. He sets up kings and removes them from power. My mind is to be fixed on Him and no other.

How about you? Have you chosen to cross the line of all these things? The Bible says that we are to love the LORD our God with all our heart, mind, soul, and strength. We are to have no other gods in our lives except the One True Living God, Jehovah. Amen.

ADDITIONAL SCRIPTURES:

"Trust in the LORD with all thine heart; and lean not unto thine own understanding. In all thy ways acknowledge him, and he shall direct thy paths."
Proverbs 3:5-6

"If any of you lack wisdom, let him ask of God, that giveth to all men liberally, and upbraideth not; and it shall be given him."
James 1:5

"Where no counsel is, the people fall: but in the multitude of counsellors there is safety."
Proverbs 11:14

"And thine ears shall hear a word behind thee, saying, This is the way, walk ye in it, when ye turn to the right hand, and when ye turn to the left."
Isaiah 30:21

"Call unto me, and I will answer thee, and shew thee great and mighty things, which thou knowest not."
Jeremiah 33:3

"I will instruct thee and teach thee in the way which thou shalt go: I will guide thee with mine eye."
Psalm 32:8

Notes:

37

Man Is Not an Animal

We hear it all the time; on the television, radio, and sometimes written in a magazine or newspaper: "Man is an animal." I am here to tell you right now that man is not an animal.

This is truly important, because the world would tear down man from his place in creation to that of just another beast. If we are just another beast, then we are as common as the beasts. In going to the creation narrative, we can see how that man is not an animal.

The first verse of the Bible simply declares God, and that He alone created from nothing the vastness of outer space and this planet we call the earth. God did not fashion the earth from other materials, He spoke it into existence from nothing. The opening verse of the Bible simply tells us that God exists, and He accomplished His will as it pleased Him.

The creation narrative further states that the earth was "void" or empty, with no life, and completely covered with water. Then God said, "Let there be light." And at His command the universe was filled with light. There was no sun, no stars, and no moon. Where did the light come from? Personally, I believe the light of the glory of God instantaneously lit and filled the universe. This is not limited by our calculated speed of light, it was instantaneous. Further, God created darkness, then separated the light from the darkness to give us day and night. All this was done on the first day.

The second day is important as God created the atmosphere of the earth. He was preparing the earth for the eventual arrival of man who would need an atmosphere which is rich with oxygen and moisture.

The third day God formed dry land on the earth, and then filled the earth with plant life. He commanded the waters to gather into places we call seas and oceans.

The fourth day God created the sun and the moon for man. They were created for our benefit to count the days, months, seasons, and years. Interestingly, God did not create anything in the sky for the week. The week is the most followed span of time for a man for it is established of God. In six days He created all things and His work was done on the seventh day. There is the week.

On the fourth day God also created the stars in five words, *"he made the stars also."* The Sovereign of the universe spoke and it was done. He also commanded the stars to shine their light on the earth, and that was instantly done as He directed.

The fifth day God filled the oceans with aquatic life of all types and the skies with all kinds of flying fowl.

The sixth day God created land animals of every kind. Up to this point, God has verbally commanded all of creation. Next He created man with a very special attention to detail.

> *"And the LORD God formed man of the dust*
> *of the ground, and breathed into his nostrils*
> *the breath of life; and man became a living*
> *soul."*
> *Genesis 2:7*

All of the animals were created by the will of God. As to the creation of man the process was different. Man was first *formed*, then God performed the first CPR, He breathed life into the man. At once, man became a living soul. The animals did not receive any of this, they were simply spoken into existence.

There are those that would say the Bible says that man is an animal. I have read these verses and they are taken out of context.

God in great wisdom created man for fellowship with Him. I have heard noted scholars try to answer, "what is the purpose of man?" King Solomon gave us the answer,

> *"Let us hear the conclusion of the whole matter: Fear God, and keep his commandments: for this is the whole duty of man."*
> *Ecclesiastes 12:13*

Not only was the creation process different for man, so is the flesh of man different compared to animals,

> *"All flesh is not the same flesh: but there is one kind of flesh of men, another flesh of beasts, another of fishes, and another of birds."*
> *I Corinthians 15:39*

Man is not an animal. The animals have instinct, but man has life breathed into him from God. Man is created in the image of God in order that we have fellowship with Him.

God gives man consciousness and life. No other creature on this planet has a place given to them as God gave man dominion over the earth.

ADDITIONAL SCRIPTURES:

"And God said, Let us make man in our image, after our likeness: and let them have dominion over the fish of the sea, and over the fowl of the air, and over the cattle, and over all the earth, and over every creeping thing that creepeth upon the earth."
Genesis 1:26

"And the fear of you and the dread of you shall be upon every beast of the earth, and upon every fowl of the air, upon all that moveth upon the earth, and upon all the fishes of the sea; into your hand are they delivered. Every moving thing that liveth shall be meat for you; even as the green herb have I given you all things."
Genesis 9:2-3

"What is man, that thou art mindful of him? and the son of man, that thou visitest him? For thou hast made him a little lower than

the angels, and hast crowned him with glory and honour. Thou madest him to have dominion over the works of thy hands; thou hast put all things under his feet:"
Psalm 8:4-6

"For in him we live, and move, and have our being; as certain also of your own poets have said, For we are also his offspring. Forasmuch then as we are the offspring of God, we ought not to think that the Godhead is like unto gold, or silver, or stone, graven by art and man's device."
Acts 17:28-29

"And have put on the new man, which is renewed in knowledge after the image of him that created him:"
Colossians 3:10

"But we all, with open face beholding as in a glass the glory of the Lord, are changed into the same image from glory to glory, even as by the Spirit of the Lord."
II Corinthians 3:18

Notes:

38

God and the Scientist

There is a joke I would like to share about a conversation between God and a scientist. The scientist was telling God that they had learned to do all the things that God could do. God then asked for a demonstration.

The scientist said he would make a man the same way God had done in Genesis 2. The scientist then knelt on the ground and began to fashion the shape of a man from the dirt. God quickly stopped the scientist and said "I made my own dirt when I made the man, you go make your own dirt."

It is very important that we as Christians carefully watch those things presented by science. I believe that scientists have accomplished many great works, but continually stray from the Word of God on matters like creation of the earth and life on the earth.

Just as someone with a sight problem will wear glasses to see clearly, we must choose the lens by which we will see spiritually. I do not view the Bible and the LORD God through the lens of science, I view science through the lens of the Bible.

When it comes to the creation narrative, I believe the Word of God as written. That God created all things in six literal days. When it comes to animal and plant life, I believe that God spoke all life into existence just as He said He did in His Word.

God is omnipotent, meaning He brings all His power to His creative ability. God created dinosaurs on the sixth day of creation. God created all the incredible varieties of birds and aquatic life on the fifth day of creation. On the sixth day of creation God created the man for the sole purpose of being in fellowship with Him.

The Bible is the recorded narrative of how God has related to man since the beginning. I believe the Bible is absolutely true and completely accurate. This faith which I have in the LORD God is a source of great peace to my life. God is in control of all things, and is also faithful to the laws of physics that He created.

Science occupies itself with many questions, many of which are difficult. Dark matter, string theory, the God particle; all have an upper level sense of knowledge to them, and might even sound important. But in my relationship with God, they are irrelevant.

My portion is to worship the Creator, the Great I Am, and to love Him with all my heart, soul, might, and mind. All the other questions I will leave to the Holy One to answer.

ADDITIONAL SCRIPTURES:

"In the beginning God created the heaven and the earth."
Genesis 1:1

"I form the light, and create darkness: I make peace, and create evil: I the LORD do all these things."
Isaiah 45:7

"For all those things hath mine hand made, and all those things have been, saith the LORD: but to this man will I look, even to him that is poor and of a contrite spirit, and trembleth at my word."
Isaiah 66:2

"Thou art worthy, O Lord, to receive glory and honour and power: for thou hast created all things, and for thy pleasure they are and were created."
Revelation 4:11

"For every creature of God is good, and nothing to be refused, if it be received with thanksgiving: For it is sanctified by the word of God and prayer."
I Timothy 4:4-5

"When I consider thy heavens, the work of thy fingers, the moon and the stars, which thou hast ordained; What is man, that thou art mindful of him? and the son of man, that thou visitest him?"
Psalm 8:3-4

Notes:

39

Things Creeping Innumerable

One of the most awe inspiring sights I have ever seen is the Texas State Aquarium in Corpus Christi, Texas. I had the privilege of visiting there on our last vacation. The experience of being there is worth more than the admission price of a ticket.

The oceans remain virtually unexplored on our planet. Scientists regularly make dives in special submarines just for the purpose of exploring a tiny bit more of our remarkable Earth. Every time they make a dive, they will discover additional species of aquatic life that we knew nothing about. Thousands of undiscovered species are found every year.

I was deeply inspired by my visit to the Texas State Aquarium for there were many exhibits displaying yet another variety of aquatic life. It reminded me of the fifth day of creation,

> *"And God said, Let the waters bring forth abundantly the moving creature that hath life, and fowl that may fly above the earth in the open firmament of heaven. And God created great whales, and every living creature that moveth, which the waters brought forth abundantly, after their kind, and every winged fowl after his kind: and God saw that it was good. And God blessed them, saying, Be fruitful, and multiply, and*

fill the waters in the seas, and let fowl
multiply in the earth. And the evening and
the morning were the fifth day."
Genesis 1:20-23

And just like that, the LORD God, the Great Creator, once again displayed His infinite creative ability for all the varieties of life that fill our oceans and skies.

"O LORD, how manifold are thy works! in
wisdom hast thou made them all: the earth
is full of thy riches."
Psalm 104:24

The psalmist stops to take notice of the marvelous creation work of God. There are so many creatures of so many different varieties, he cannot number them all. I believe the Psalmist is overwhelmed by the Great Creator, and then says,

"So is this great and wide sea, wherein are
things creeping innumerable, both small
and great beasts."
Psalm 104:25

In the day over three thousand years ago when Psalm 104 was written, man knew very little about the oceans. But because the scriptures are inspired of God, the Psalmist knew of God to write this verse. So now we do not have to wonder, God has explained to us that the oceans of the air and of the sea are filled with life created by Him.

One day, if I have the opportunity, I would once again like to visit the Texas State Aquarium. It was a pleasure to see the dolphins, sharks, and star fish. We were able to feed and touch small manta rays which were on display. They even had a sea turtle that was rescued due to an injury and he peacefully swims about in his tank.

All varieties of life, in all their infinite splendor, created by the LORD God.

ADDITIONAL SCRIPTURES:

"Through faith we understand that the worlds were framed by the word of God, so that things which are seen were not made of things which do appear."
Hebrews 11:3

"The earth is the LORD'S, and the fullness thereof; the world, and they that dwell therein."
Psalm 24:1

"For every beast of the forest is mine, and the cattle upon a thousand hills. I know all the fowls of the mountains: and the wild beasts of the field are mine."
Psalm 50:10-11

"Behold the fowls of the air: for they sow

not, neither do they reap, nor gather into barns; yet your heavenly Father feedeth them. Are ye not much better than they?"
Matthew 6:26

"He giveth to the beast his food, and to the young ravens which cry."
Psalm 147:9

"They give drink to every beast of the field: the wild asses quench their thirst. By them shall the fowls of the heaven have their habitation, which sing among the branches."
Psalm 104:11-12

Notes:

The Deepest Part of Your Heart

Listening is an acquired skill. Since I'm a preacher, there have been several instances where people wanted to talk, and the more they talk the inner secrets of the heart begin to reveal themselves. These inner secrets begin to surface as the talker develops a trust with the listener; that these secrets will be kept.

Secrets are a precious thing, dear to the owner of the secret. Sometimes these deep secrets are not revealed because of shame or embarrassment. These are the secrets kept in the deepest part of your heart. We are not speaking about the muscle in your chest which pumps blood, but the inner most part of your being, that part of who you are.

I want you to know that no matter the secret you carry, no matter the burden, you can take it to God. There is a part of us that would rather share with someone who has skin on, but there is also a greater risk the one with the skin will publicize your secret.

We honor God when we take everything to Him, no matter what it is.

> *"Cast thy burden upon the LORD, and he shall sustain thee: he shall never suffer the righteous to be moved."*
> *Psalm 55:22*

God is an excellent listener. Even though He is

omniscient and already knows the deepest part of your heart, He is pleased whenever we reveal those secret things to Him. It is an admission of trust in Him that He will keep these things which makes our faith stronger in Him.

> *"For the word of the LORD is right; and all*
> *his works are done in truth. He loveth*
> *righteousness and judgment: the earth is*
> *full of the goodness of the Lord."*
> *Psalm 33: 4-5*

I like Psalm 37 where the writer, under the inspiration of God, tells us that this is a three step process.

First of all, we are to trust in God. Actually, trusting in God is a recurring theme throughout scripture. We can trust God concerning creation, and Noah's Flood; we can trust Him concerning His promises and covenants, and finally we can trust Him with the salvation of our souls.

> *"Trust in the LORD, and do good; so shalt*
> *thou dwell in the land, and verily thou shalt*
> *be fed."*
> *Psalm 37:3*

Secondly, we are to delight ourselves in the LORD. This means that we are to continually expect all our happiness to come from Him. We should delight in everything as it relates to the Father, the Son, and the Holy Spirit. It pleases the LORD God to then supply those things we desire as we delight in Him.

*"Delight thyself also in the LORD; and he
shall give thee the desires of thine heart."*
Psalm 37:4

And third, we are to commit unto the LORD. The scriptures say specifically we are to commit *our way* unto the LORD. When we take all our cares and the deepest things of our heart and give them to Him, God takes over and carries the load.

*"Commit thy way unto the LORD; trust also
in him; and he shall bring it to pass."*
Psalm 37:5

Perhaps it is time that you would share with God the secret things in the deepest part of your heart. He is with you now, and waiting for you to yield those secret things to Him. He will be very pleased at the faith and trust you place in Him.

ADDITIONAL SCRIPTURES:

*"Offer the sacrifices of righteousness, and
put your trust in the LORD."*
Psalm 4:5

*"Blessed is the man that trusteth in the
LORD, and whose hope the LORD is."*
Jeremiah 17:7

"Then will I go unto the altar of God, unto God my exceeding joy: yea, upon the harp will I praise thee, O God my God."
Psalm 43:4

"Then shalt thou delight thyself in the LORD; and I will cause thee to ride upon the high places of the earth, and feed thee with the heritage of Jacob thy father: for the mouth of the LORD hath spoken it."
Isaiah 58:14

"Whom having not seen, ye love; in whom, though now ye see him not, yet believing, ye rejoice with joy unspeakable and full of glory:"
I Peter 1:8

"Commit thy works unto the LORD, and thy thoughts shall be established."
Proverbs 16:3

Notes:

41

Measure Twice – Cut Once

Occasionally I have the pleasure of working in my woodshop. Most of the time I will work with common domestic hardwoods such as red oak, ash, and maple. These woods are moderately priced and I exercise care not to make a mistake and ruin the wood. If I do make a mistake the loss is bearable because the wood is not that expensive. I simply go to the woodpile and get another piece.

There are times when I work with foreign exotic woods that are very expensive, sometimes costing as much as 100 dollars per board-foot. It is these times when I will measure the wood carefully and then measure again before cutting the wood with the saw. One wrong cut can ruin the piece of wood forever.

The *measure twice, cut once* saying is sound advice, whether you are cutting wood or making a decision for your life. Obviously, your life is not a piece of wood; your life is very valuable. The decisions you make are like measuring a piece of wood. You need to think things through twice before taking action or *making the cut.* Once the cut is made, it is final. Sometimes our decisions can lead to dire consequences.

In Proverbs chapter 19:21 we have these words,

> *"There are many devices in a man's heart; nevertheless the counsel of the LORD, that shall stand."*

The secret here is we need the counsel of the LORD in our hearts so when decision time comes, to make the *cut* in the wood as it were, we would make the decision in accordance with His wisdom.

God, in His wisdom, gave us instruction on how to live our lives. However, I have found that many are not interested in what God has to say. This attitude in man is addressed in Proverbs chapter 14:12,

> *"There is a way which seemeth right unto a man, but the end thereof are the ways of death."*

These people whose way seems right to themselves do so because it serves themselves. It provides the moments of gain or pleasure they are seeking.

I mentioned earlier that your life is valuable. And it is. I pray you will place a high value on your life and make those decisions which are best for you and honoring unto God.

ADDITIONAL SCRIPTURES:

> *"Rejoicing in hope; patient in tribulation; continuing instant in prayer;"*
> Romans 12:12

> *"But when that which is perfect is come, then that which is in part shall be done*

away."
I Corinthians 13:10

"Thou wilt shew me the path of life: in thy presence is fulness of joy; at thy right hand there are pleasures for evermore."
Psalm 16:11

"But his delight is in the law of the LORD; and in his law doth he meditate day and night."
Psalm 1:2

"The law of the LORD is perfect, converting the soul: the testimony of the LORD is sure, making wise the simple."
Psalm 19:7

"The statutes of the LORD are right, rejoicing the heart: the commandment of the LORD is pure, enlightening the eyes."
Psalm 19:8

Notes:

42

The Indolence of Leaving the Stump

People chop down trees for many reasons. Some are diseased, others are damaged by the wind of a storm, and others are damaged by a lightning strike. Sometimes a tree must be removed for building a house or to make way for a driveway. Felling the tree is the easy part. Modern chain saws can make quick work of taking a tree from vertical to horizontal. Then the felled tree must have the limbs removed and the trunk of the tree cut into pieces small enough to haul way. Then there is the matter of the stump.

On the campus of First Baptist Church in Roxton we had a couple of trees which were removed, but the stumps are still there. Around Roxton there are several stumps that have never been removed. Perhaps the plan was to allow the stump to rot, which is the long approach to the problem.

Truth is, a tree stump is unsightly, especially in an otherwise beautiful yard. You have to mow around it, rake around it, and so on. It is always in the way. When the stump is not dead, new sprouts will emerge as the roots nourish new growth. If left alone, in time to come, the stump will produce new growth that has to be dealt with as before.

Sometimes I think of a tree stump like a sign of sin. Moved by the Word of God to take care of sin, a human will often chop down the tree without removing the stump. Stump removal becomes the hard part. One has to admit that removing a stump, physical or spiritual, can be a lot of work. So often-times they are left behind, hoping enough work has been done to take care of the problem. But it is there, virtually unmovable.

Sin has a way of snaring and devouring us. Remember always the devil planned it that way. In First Peter chapter 5 and verse 8,

"Be sober, be vigilant; because your
adversary the devil, as a roaring lion,
walketh about, seeking whom he may
devour:"

The devil appears to give you a good life, but that is the trap. Once lured into sin, it takes over, and then you are devoured or destroyed by it.

When the Children of Israel began to conquer the Promised Land, God gave instructions that they were to completely destroy the inhabitants of the land. This might seem cruel to the carnal man, but God is Sovereign and in His righteous omniscience knew if Israel did not completely remove the inhabitants and their idolatry, that Israel would be continually in the snare of idol worship.

"They shall not dwell in thy land, lest they
make thee sin against me: for if thou serve
their gods, it will surely be a snare unto
thee."
Exodus 23:33

To solve the problem by chopping down the tree and leaving the stump is exactly what the devil wants you to do. You can't see them, but the stump has roots. If the roots remain alive the stump will sprout new growth. The problem returns.

ADDITIONAL SCRIPTURES:

"If we confess our sins, he is faithful and just to forgive us our sins, and to cleanse us from all unrighteousness."
I John 1:9

"This I say then, Walk in the Spirit, and ye shall not fulfil the lust of the flesh."
Galatians 5:16

"What shall we say then? Shall we continue in sin, that grace may abound?"
Romans 6:1

"What then? shall we sin, because we are not under the law, but under grace? God forbid."
Romans 6:15

"Then saith Jesus unto him, Get thee hence, Satan: for it is written, Thou shalt worship the Lord thy God, and him only shalt thou serve."
Matthew 4:10

"For there are certain men crept in unawares, who were before of old ordained to this condemnation, ungodly men, turning the grace of our God into lasciviousness, and denying the only Lord God, and our Lord Jesus Christ."
Jude 1:4

Notes:

43

A Case for the Fire Breathing Dragon

Some Christians have a hard time when they read Job 41. This particular chapter is used exclusively to describe a wild and fierce animal which lives in the water, and can expel fire. We could call this animal a fire breathing dragon. It sounds like a fairy tale of sorts with knights in shining armor, fair maidens, and ancient castles.

To begin with, I believe the translators of the scripture accurately translated Job chapter 41. And since all scripture is given by inspiration of God, and our great Creator is completely reliable and truthful in His Word, let's make a case for this fire breathing, or more accurately, fire expelling dragon.

These dragons are mentioned occasionally in scripture. The name "Leviathan" simply means something very large and powerful. The early Bible scholars believed the leviathan was one of several different types of animals, including possibly the crocodile, the whale, or some other type of large fish which had teeth.

"There go the ships: there is that leviathan,
whom thou hast made to play therein."
Psalm 104:26

When we once again search the scriptures we see the complete description of this animal in Job chapter 41. When God begins in verse 1 of this chapter to describe the animal, there is an implied familiarity that Job has had a glimpse of the animal before. Probably there were also stories from the early mariners of such a beast.

As God questions Job about this beast, we also learn of the incredible creative ability of God.

Job, can you draw out leviathan with a hook? Job knew how to fish, and the impossibility of landing this beast to the shore, partly due to his size, and his fierceness was very evident.

Job, will the leviathan ask you to let him go? Will he bargain with you? Again, the leviathan is a huge, wild, and fierce beast. To tangle with this beast would be a great battle.

Job, can you play with a leviathan like you play with a caged bird? Job, can you make it a pet for your daughter? God is revealing that the LORD God can control this beast, and Job can't.

Then God had the writer of Job, who is unknown, reveal to us that this magnificent beast breathes fire,

> *"Out of his mouth go burning lamps, and sparks of fire leap out. Out of his nostrils goeth smoke, as out of a seething pot or caldron. His breath kindleth coals, and a flame goeth out of his mouth."*
> *Job 41:19-21*

The last time I looked, neither the whale nor the crocodile is a fire breathing animal. I can hear you now, "Bro. Louis, you have gone too far." Okay, I agree this will push a lot of Christians out of their comfort zone. But shall we review what we learned in school?

I know of no one that doubts the existence of the firefly. When the mating time comes for this creature in summer its abdomen will glow to attract a mate, yet he is unharmed by the flashing of light.

Do you doubt the existence of the electric eel? How is it possible that this animal can come close and discharge a significant amount of electricity to catch its prey? Yet the eel is unharmed?

Have you ever heard of the angler fish who will attract its prey in the depths of the ocean with a glowing bulb attached to the end of a long growth on its head?

Have you heard of the bombardier beetle? It stores in its body two different chemicals that can be combined as a powerful defense mechanism. They are released into a chamber of the abdomen and will rise rapidly in temperature, then expel the explosive mixture towards their enemy. Sometimes the blast can be fatal.

No one doubts the poison carried by various snakes whose bite can be deadly, yet the snake is not harmed by the poison it carries in its body. The same principle applies to the bee or the wasp. Many of us have experienced the wrath of a nest of wasps. The sting can really smart.

Even the familiar skunk can spray its attacker with a very powerful smell that one will not soon forget, yet the skunk will bask in the musk he emits.

I have faith that God would have no problem making a wild and fierce aquatic creature capable of combining two different organic compounds which once combined and expelled would produce smoke and fire.

"Is anything too hard for the LORD?"
Genesis 18:14a

Man has long used two different compounds that are combustible once combined for a variety of purposes. The German Luftwaffe used two different compounds mixed together to power a small rocket plane known as the Messerschmitt ME163 to prey on and destroy Allied bombers during World War Two. Also, NASA used similar types of propellants for the Gemini program back in the 1960's as we prepared to make a journey to the moon.

As far as we know the Leviathan is extinct. As man developed the technologies to kill this creature I am sure they were hunted as a great prize. Would you believe if we had a sample of this creature on display?

The same thing goes for the Bible. We do not have the original copy. God has preserved His Word for us using the skills of knowledgeable men. If we had the original copy of the Bible there would be those who would worship it.

It is by faith we believe.

"For by grace are ye saved through faith;"
Ephesians 2:8a

We have no monuments, no artifacts, just memories of special places (like Jerusalem) and the written Word of God. Ours is a life of faith. Embrace it and live it.

ADDITIONAL SCRIPTURES:

"In that day the LORD with his sore and great and strong sword shall punish leviathan the piercing serpent, even leviathan that crooked serpent; and he shall slay the dragon that is in the sea."
Isaiah 27:1

"Thou brakest the heads of leviathan in pieces, and gavest him to be meat to the people inhabiting the wilderness."
Psalm 74:14

"Thou didst divide the sea by thy strength: thou brakest the heads of the dragons in the waters."
Psalm 74:13

"And he laid hold on the dragon, that old serpent, which is the Devil, and Satan, and bound him a thousand years,"
Revelation 20:2

"There go the ships: there is that leviathan, whom thou hast made to play therein. These wait all upon thee; that thou mayest give them their meat in due season."
Psalm 104:26-27

"Upon earth there is not his like, who is

made without fear."
Job 41:33

Notes:

44

The Criteria of a Canon

The Bible is the most precious book for the believer. As Christians, our faith begins with the Scriptures and their authority. Believe it or not, there was a time when man did not have the Bible. From the time of Creation to the time of Moses, man did not have written documents inspired of God. It wasn't until the late 1400's when the printing press made it possible to print multiple copies of the scriptures.

The first five books of the Bible are called the Pentateuch. This is a Greek word that means "five scrolls:" the writing of Moses. In it, God gave the eye witness accounts of Creation, early civilizations, the flood, and the history of Abraham, Isaac, and Jacob. We also have the Law as given by God.

Others wrote as moved by the Spirit of God, so we get the history of the conquering of Canaan, the lives of David, Solomon, and the Kings of Israel and Judah. The Old Testament also has the writings of prophets like Jeremiah, Ezekiel, Daniel, and many others.

When Jesus lived and died in Judea there were books written about His life, then the actions of the Apostles, and finally the writing of the Apostles.

In the 4th century A.D. the Scriptures were canonized into a single book which we now call the Bible. It is considered a *closed* canon; no book can be added and none taken away. The Old Testament was pretty much established when Jesus was on the earth. It was the New

Testament that was to be canonized. There were four criteria for a book to be canonized into the New Testament. They were as follows:

     1.   *Apostolic Origin — attributed to and based upon the preaching/teaching of the first-generation apostles.*
     2.   *Universal Acceptance — acknowledged by all major Christian communities in the ancient world (by the end of the 4th century) as well as accepted canon by Jewish authorities (for the Old Testament).*
     3.   *Liturgical Use — read publicly when early Christian communities gathered for the Lord's Supper (their weekly worship services).*
     4. *Consistent Message — containing a theological outlook similar to or complementary to other accepted Christian writings.*

The Bible is a miracle in itself. The Old and New Testaments were written by nearly 40 different authors over a period of about 2000 years, yet it is in agreement. The Apostle Paul wrote these great words about the Bible:

> *"All scripture is given by inspiration of God,*
> *and is profitable for doctrine, for reproof,*
> *for correction, for instruction in*
> *righteousness:"*
> *II Timothy 3:16*

I have a book in my library titled "The Lost Books of

the Bible", which highlights books discovered later on that are not in the canon of scriptures. I am sure that after Christ ascended into heaven that many took it upon themselves to write spiritual books. There are many, but, none are canonized.

I have the faith that God would move to preserve His word here on this earth. I think it is wonderful that we have the Bible as it is, nothing more needed, nothing to be taken away.

> *"For ever, O LORD, thy word is settled in*
> *heaven."*
> *Psalm 119:89*

I believe that God moved in the hearts of men to gather the writings and *canonize* them for His Glory. The books which belong in the Bible are there; books which do not belong are not included.

The Bible is our Authority for faith and practice. We must spend time in the Word, allowing the Living Word of God to feed our souls. The Bible is a marvelous gift from God. Read it every chance you get.

ADDITIONAL SCRIPTURES:

> *"Is not my word like as a fire? saith the*
> *LORD; and like a hammer that breaketh the*
> *rock in pieces?"*
> *Jeremiah 23:29*

> *"For the word of God is quick, and powerful,*

*and sharper than any two-edged sword,
piercing even to the dividing asunder of soul
and spirit, and of the joints and marrow,
and is a discerner of the thoughts and
intents of the heart."*
Hebrews 4:12

*"And they said one to another, Did not our
heart burn within us, while he talked with us
by the way, and while he opened to us the
scriptures?"*
Luke 24:32

*"Therefore I love thy commandments above
gold; yea, above fine gold."*
Psalm 119:127

*"Open thou mine eyes, that I may behold
wondrous things out of thy law."*
Psalm 119:18

*"That the God of our Lord Jesus Christ, the
Father of glory, may give unto you the spirit
of wisdom and revelation in the knowledge
of him:"*
Ephesians 1:17

Notes:

45

Prudence Hoskinson and the Knitting Lesson

When I was about fifteen years old there was an elderly lady in our church in Grapevine that lived just down the street on the corner. Prudence was smitten with my Mom and Dad and would walk a few yards up the street to the parsonage to visit from time to time.

Prudence Hoskinson was born in Elizabethtown, Kentucky, in 1896. She was about five-foot-nothin' high, wore very old fashioned clothes that she made herself, and tied her hair in a silver gray bun on top of her head. She had a hard time keeping her glasses in place because her narrow nose would allow them to slide down all the time. She was always up for a good laugh.

There was a running joke between my parents and Prudence. One of the staple foods we ate all the time was pinto beans and cornbread. I don't know who started it, but there was always laughter about how the beans were cooked and whether or not the cornbread was too dry.

Eventually there was a friendship that grew between Prudence and me. I think it started when I would go to her small house to mow her yard. She didn't have much money so there were a few times I would accept a book of *Green Stamps* for mowing her yard. She always insisted on paying me so I graciously accepted what she wanted to do.

I would help her with occasional chores around the house, and take her to town for shopping. I think that people began to talk because of the 61-year difference in our ages, but the girls I knew at church and school didn't seem to mind!

During the winter it was not easy for Prudence to walk up the street to visit with my parents so I would walk to her house for a visit. She always offered me coffee or tea, and we would sit close to her Dearborn heater and visit. She loved to talk about how she was raised and the values she learned in her life. We would talk about family, friends, and how she loved my parents and the church. Those cold winter evenings were a lot easier to pass in the presence of good company.

One time I went down for a visit and Prudence was knitting. I was intrigued since I had never before watched anyone knit. I had watched my mother crochet, but this knitting thing was really neat. The knitting needles were really large compared to the crochet needle; the yarn was thicker and it appeared it was easier to make progress on a project.

I think Prudence could tell I was interested so she asked me if I would like to try knitting myself. I enthusiastically said *yes*! Before I knew it I was holding another pair of knitting needles and a ball of golden yarn.

Prudence had me watch her as she would loop the yarn over one needle and pull it through with the other needle. She kept repeating the process and moments later she had completed the first row. Then I tried...loop and pull, loop and pull. Hey, there was nothing too this!

Row by row I knit my first scarf, perfect for those cold winter walks to see Prudence. As I was knitting along I added a third step that Prudence did not teach me, you see, I would loop, pull, and tug tightly. OK, I'm a man, I thought it would make it better! Well, Prudence wanted to show me another stitch so she asked me for my needles and work. My stitches were so tight she could hardly do anything with what I had done. "Why did you pull these stitches so tight?" she said with a flustered voice. I really didn't have an answer. I was honestly proud of what I had accomplished.

Just like I added an extra step to the knitting lesson, many people have added extra, unnecessary steps to their relationship with God. The relationship with God is intended to be simple. God is holy, and the relationship must be on His terms.

Don't make it complicated. If you do, He will never be able to show you something new.

ADDITIONAL SCRIPTURES:

"But God commendeth his love toward us, in that, while we were yet sinners, Christ died for us."
Romans 5:8

"If we confess our sins, he is faithful and just to forgive us our sins, and to cleanse us from all unrighteousness."
I John 1:9

"Behold, I stand at the door, and knock: if any man hear my voice, and open the door, I will come in to him, and will sup with him, and he with me."

Revelation 3:20

"Draw nigh to God, and he will draw nigh to you."
James 4:8

"For I know the thoughts that I think toward you, saith the LORD, thoughts of peace, and not of evil, to give you an expected end. Then shall ye call upon me, and ye shall go and pray unto me, and I will hearken unto you."
Jeremiah 29:11-12

"But without faith it is impossible to please him: for he that cometh to God must believe that he is, and that he is a rewarder of them that diligently seek him."
Hebrews 11:6

Notes:

46

Recognizing God's Provision

There is a story of heavy rains and rising flood waters so the local fire departments were trying to take people to the safety of higher ground. The rescuers had a boat going from house to house that brought the residents to safety.

As the story goes, one man was approached by the rescuers and they asked him if he would like a ride to safety. The man assured the rescuers that everything was okay. "God is going to rescue me!" he boasted.

The waters continued to rise and the fire department sent the boat by a second time to persuade the man to abandon the house and move to safety. They found the waters had risen significantly and the man was sitting on the edge of his roof. But, again the man refused while assuring the rescuers, "God is going to rescue me!"

The dangers were becoming great as the waters continued to rise. The boat was sent the third time to rescue the stubborn man. They found him on the uppermost ridge of his roof, the waves lapping at his shoes. "Would you like a ride to safety?" the rescuers inquired? "NO!" the man exclaimed, "God is going to rescue me!"

Eventually the waters rose and completely covered his house and the man was swept away.

When the man awoke he was standing before God. You would think the man would be glad to be in the presence of the Creator, but, alas, he was very upset.

"LORD, I told those firemen that you were going to rescue me! How can you let me die in a flood like that?" Then God replied, "I sent the boat by three times!"

Our all-knowing God is aware of the life of every individual on the earth. He knows just what you need in good times and bad. Sometimes man has a difficult time recognizing the provision of God in their lives. I believe this happens most when God provides what you need rather than what you want. There is a difference.

I recently experienced God's provision. It was a rainy Monday morning and I was on my 40-mile drive to work. As I was leaving Roxton a hunger overwhelmed me so I decided to stop at the Roxton Café to get a breakfast biscuit. The sausage biscuits they make are really good, especially if you put a slice of cheese on the sausage.

The stopping and purchasing of the sausage biscuit and the associated conversation in the café cost me some time, about ten minutes.

About two thirds of the way to work I drove up on an accident that took the lives of three people. The accident was a head-on collision caused by one vehicles' excessive speed and hydroplaning into the oncoming lane. It happened about 10 minutes before I got there. The accident was going to happen, God just made sure I was not a part of it.

My only conclusion is that God still has work for me to perform. I'd best get busy about the Masters business.

ADDITIONAL SCRIPTURES:

"But my God shall supply all your need according to his riches in glory by Christ Jesus."
Philippians 4:19

"The LORD is my shepherd; I shall not want."
Psalm 23:1

"Being confident of this very thing, that he which hath begun a good work in you will perform it until the day of Jesus Christ:"
Philippians 1:6

"Ask, and it shall be given you; seek, and ye shall find; knock, and it shall be opened unto you: For every one that asketh receiveth; and he that seeketh findeth; and to him that knocketh it shall be opened."
Matthew 7:7-8

"And God is able to make all grace abound toward you; that ye, always having all sufficiency in all things, may abound to every good work:"
II Corinthians 9:8

"Let your conversation be without covetousness; and be content with such

things as ye have: for he hath said, I will never leave thee, nor forsake thee"
Hebrews 13:5

Notes:

47

The Favorite Book

Many years ago I heard the joke of the preacher visiting a lady, encouraging her to have a closer walk with God by reading her Bible. So the story goes she assured the preacher that her Bible was indeed her favorite book and then turned to her little boy and said, "Son, go to the bedroom and bring mommies' favorite book so I can show the preacher." The boy disappeared down the hallway and soon returned to his mother, proudly carrying the latest Sears and Roebuck catalog!

While the best of intentions seemed to backfire on the lady, there is an inconvenient truth here; as a rule, we as a people spend precious little time in the Word of God.

In fact, we as a nation spend little time reading at all. I found a recent article which said the average American spends less than 19 minutes a day reading. Young adults spend even less time, about 8 minutes. Also, a recent survey found that most American adults are below average in reading skills, especially compared to other developed nations. America was beat out by Japan, South Korea, and Australia among others.

It seems like an uphill battle for a preacher to be asking folks to read the Bible, but I guess I am an optimist.

I am not a betting man, but I would propose that the majority of homes in Roxton have a Bible in them. It might be shelved on a bookcase or sitting on the coffee table, but I believe they are there. Don't you believe it is time to put them to good use?

The Bible seems to be too hard to read. If you believe *that* then the devil has you right where he wants you. The devil knows if you read the Bible you will learn truth. He does not want that to happen.

The Bible is a marvelous miracle of God. It is not a book you read once for pleasure and then shelve, but rather it is a book of God's truth that brings the joy of knowing the Creator. Refer to it often.

ADDITIONAL SCRIPTURES:

"Thy word is a lamp unto my feet, and a light unto my path."
Psalm 119:105

"For the commandment is a lamp; and the law is light; and reproofs of instruction are the way of life:"
Proverbs 6:23

"But he answered and said, It is written, Man shall not live by bread alone, but by every word that proceedeth out of the mouth of God."
Matthew 4:4

"For whatsoever things were written aforetime were written for our learning, that we through patience and comfort of the scriptures might have hope."
Romans 15:4

"But his delight is in the law of the LORD; and in his law doth he meditate day and night."
Psalm 1:2

"In the beginning was the Word, and the Word was with God, and the Word was God."
John 1:1

Notes:

48

The Battle of the Bulge

It was a beautiful sunny afternoon in Grapevine Texas, and I was in my room working on another project. I could hear the noises of construction across the street as the men worked on the new auditorium for the church. All of a sudden, there was a huge crash of something falling down. It was not the sound of metal or wood crashing together, it was rock and stone.

On the end of the new church building facing the street, was a rock face to accent the red brick. The brick had already been laid, and all that was left for the bricklayer was the rock fascia as decoration. The bricklayer was almost done when the rock face was pushed away from the building and it crashed to the ground. Thank the LORD God that no one was hurt!

The bricklayer readily admitted what went wrong. As he was building the rock face he had extra bricks and rock to do something with so he inserted the unneeded material behind the rock face next to the inside wall of the building. The extra weight began to build, and then it began to push outward on the freshly laid rock, until enough weight built up and the rock face gave way. He lost the battle of the bulge.

Your life can be thought of as a beautiful rock face. If you have extra junk materials that you are also trying to carry, it can build up to the point that your beautiful rock face will crash. For the sake of illustration let's call the extra material sin. Just as the rock face on the church did not need the extra material pushing from behind, so your life, your beautiful rock face does not need sin pushing from the inside out.

The Apostle Paul wrote these encouraging words in Hebrews Chapter 12:1-2,

"Wherefore seeing we also are compassed about with so great a cloud of witnesses, let us lay aside every weight, and the sin which doth so easily beset us, and let us run with patience the race that is set before us, Looking unto Jesus the author and finisher of our faith;"

I heard a great evangelist tell the story of how he ran a race when he was a little boy. Art Wilson was a bit short, and it would be easy to imagine him in boy's overalls. With all the many pockets of his overalls loaded with treasures he said he would start at the top to empty them, working his way down. There would be firecrackers, frogs, a lizard, a toy car, and a pop gun, marbles, a nickel, so forth. He was illustrating just how important it was to be a light as possible for the race. He was removing anything that might bulge.

After things were cleaned up, the bricklayer once again put up the rock face, carefully choosing each stone to mortar into place. The rock fascia was again put into place, but this time no extra materials were hidden behind by the bricklayer.

This time we had knowledge and wisdom to apply to the building of the rock face, and it is there to this day.

ADDITIONAL SCRIPTURES:

"For I know that in me (that is, in my flesh,) dwelleth no good thing: for to will is present with me; but how to perform that which is good I find not."
Romans 7:18

"Dearly beloved, I beseech you as strangers and pilgrims, abstain from fleshly lusts, which war against the soul;"
I Peter 2:11

"This I say then, Walk in the Spirit, and ye shall not fulfil the lust of the flesh."
Galatians 5:16

"For they that are after the flesh do mind the things of the flesh; but they that are after the Spirit the things of the Spirit. For to be carnally minded is death; but to be spiritually minded is life and peace."
Romans 8:5-6

"Then said Jesus to those Jews which believed on him, If ye continue in my word, then are ye my disciples indeed;
And ye shall know the truth, and the truth shall make you free."
John 8:31-32

"But every man is tempted, when he is drawn away of his own lust, and enticed. Then when lust hath conceived, it bringeth forth sin: and sin, when it is finished, bringeth forth death."
James 1:14-15

Notes:

49

A Day on Uncle Blicky's Farm

Many years ago my parents would go to visit Mom's uncle, Clarence Roberts, who owned a remote farm in far southeastern Oklahoma. He was my Grandmother Holt's younger brother. He was known as Uncle Blicky because as a young child he had once tasted soured milk and pronounced it as *blinky* which in time evolved into "Blicky" as a nickname which stayed with him all his life.

Uncle Blicky and Aunt Ruth loved it when kinfolks came, but one had to be careful when going to their house. He kept a loaded shotgun by the door, and if there was a knock on the door in the night, the first thing the visitor would meet is the business end of Uncle Blicky's shotgun.

Retired from actively farming, Uncle Blicky spent his time taking care of his place and the animals. One day, he was showing my Dad around the farm when they came upon a spring fed pond full of catfish. Uncle Blicky also fed them every day. Dad asked if he ever tried to catch the catfish; Uncle Blicky said he hadn't. He then invited Dad to come and fish the pond anytime he wanted. Dad knew that all the catfish had seen was the catfish chow they were fed on a daily basis. If some good ripe blood bait was put on a treble hook the possibility was very good for a catch. Furthermore, since the pond had never been fished, the fish would be a nice size.

Uncle Blicky was very diligent to feed every animal

on the farm from the big Brahma bull that ate out of his hand to the pigs, chickens, ducks, cats, dogs, and those catfish in the pond. Uncle Blicky said emphatically, "There ain't nothing going to bed hungry on this farm."

Dad knew his grandchildren would have a good time catching the fish so we were invited to go to Uncle Blicky's farm for a day of fishing and good time. My children were very excited about the day and off we went.

The main attraction at the farm was the fishing. It was great fun as the catfish would waste no time in biting the hook with the tasty bait. Anyone with a line in the pond caught a fish. My children loved every minute of it.

One thing about a farm is that the food can be absolutely wonderful. For lunch that afternoon, Aunt Ruth brought out a big tray of sliced vine ripe tomatoes and several ears of fresh corn, all prepared to perfection.

The folks at First Baptist in Roxton will tell you that I absolutely love home grown tomatoes. I quickly filled my plate with several choice slices of tomatoes and an ear of corn, buttered and seasoned for a feast.

One of the most special events for the Christian is when we first get to heaven for the marriage supper of the Lamb. The Lord Himself has a feast planned for His church which is a future event that we cannot imagine. It will be truly "out of this world" for it will be in heaven.

Jesus gave us an example in Matthew chapter 22,

*"The kingdom of heaven is like unto a
certain king, which made a marriage for his
son, And sent forth his servants to call them*

that were bidden to the wedding: and they
would not come. Again, he sent forth other
servants, saying, Tell them which are
bidden, Behold, I have prepared my dinner:
my oxen and my fatlings are killed, and all
things are ready: come unto the marriage.
But they made light of it, and went their
ways, one to his farm, another to his
merchandise:"
Matthew 22:2-5

The LORD God is very proud of His Son Jesus Christ. Everyone in the world has received an invitation to the marriage supper, but there are many who will chose not to come. One thing we must be careful of is the Father's love for the Son. God the Father loves His only begotten Son very much. God does not take it lightly when men will mock His Son.

When Jesus was baptized the LORD God spoke these words,

"And Jesus, when he was baptized, went up
straightway out of the water: and, lo, the
heavens were opened unto him, and he saw
the Spirit of God descending like a dove, and
lighting upon him: And lo a voice from
heaven, saying, This is my beloved Son, in
whom I am well pleased."
Matthew 3:16-17

Further, God has set His Son on high with a great

name:

"Wherefore God also hath highly exalted
him, and given him a name which is above
every name: That at the name of Jesus
every knee should bow, of things in heaven,
and things in earth, and things under the
earth; And that every tongue should confess
that Jesus Christ is Lord, to the glory of God
the Father."
Philippians 2:9-11

One has to realize just how much God the Father esteems His Son. Next, everyone has been invited to the marriage supper of the Lamb. God has made sure everyone knows they are invited. For those who reject the offer and will not come, God has reserved judgment for them in outer darkness. God loves His Son that much.

I don't know if we will have sliced home grown tomatoes and corn-on-the–cob at the marriage supper of the Lamb, but if we do, I have already had a sample.

ADDITIONAL SCRIPTURES:

"And if I go and prepare a place for you, I
will come again, and receive you unto
myself; that where I am, there ye may be
also."
John 14:3

"And I heard as it were the voice of a great

multitude, and as the voice of many waters, and as the voice of mighty thunderings, saying, Alleluia: for the Lord God omnipotent reigneth. Let us be glad and rejoice, and give honour to him: for the marriage of the Lamb is come, and his wife hath made herself ready. And to her was granted that she should be arrayed in fine linen, clean and white: for the fine linen is the righteousness of saints. And he saith unto me, Write, Blessed are they which are called unto the marriage supper of the Lamb. And he saith unto me, These are the true sayings of God."
Revelation 19:6-9

"Watch therefore, for ye know neither the day nor the hour wherein the Son of man cometh."
Matthew 25:13

"But thou shalt go unto my country, and to my kindred, and take a wife unto my son Isaac."
Genesis 24:4

"For thy Maker is thine husband; the LORD of hosts is his name; and thy Redeemer the Holy One of Israel; The God of the whole earth shall he be called."
Isaiah 54:5

"Behold, I shew you a mystery; We shall not all sleep, but we shall all be changed, In a moment, in the twinkling of an eye, at the last trump: for the trumpet shall sound, and the dead shall be raised incorruptible, and we shall be changed. For this corruptible must put on incorruption, and this mortal must put on immortality."
I Corinthians 15:51-53

Notes:

50

The Chicken and the Egg

It is a question that has puzzled humanity since ages ago. We ask the question once again, not to debate the question, but to seek truth from the Word of God.

So, which came first, the chicken or the egg?

For the truth we must turn to the Word of God. In Genesis Chapter 1 we read about the fifth day of creation which says,

"And God said, Let the waters bring forth abundantly the moving creature that hath life, and fowl that may fly above the earth in the open firmament of heaven. And God created great whales, and every living creature that moveth, which the waters brought forth abundantly, after their kind, and every winged fowl after his kind: and God saw that it was good. And God blessed them, saying, Be fruitful, and multiply, and fill the waters in the seas, and let fowl multiply in the earth. And the evening and the morning were the fifth day."
Genesis 1:20-23

The chicken is a winged fowl that does not specialize in flying. I have seen a chicken, startled, flap its wings to hop across the yard and that is about it. Perhaps in the day's right after creation they were better fliers.

However, the scripture is specific that winged fowl, not the egg, was created on the fifth day.

The fertilized egg itself is a marvel of creation. Contained within its shell is the life of another chick. Jan and I have small birds called cockatiels that have laid and hatched a clutch of eggs. When the chicks hatch out they are complete as they begin their new life. To make a cockatiel a pet, the chicks must be taken away from the mother hen at about 2 weeks and be hand-fed until they are weaned. Jan and I are getting older so we do not raise the chicks any more, but even a few years ago, the feedings at 2 and 6 am were tough.

It isn't long though and the chicks can go all night without a feeding. What's remarkable is that their feathers begin to grow and mature. The chicks like to eat, then sit on a perch to practice flapping their wings. And suddenly when they are about 6 weeks old, they will be practicing their wing flapping only to let go of the perch. All of a sudden, this young chick is flying around the house like a butterfly. The flight is totally unauthorized and totally unexpected, but they fly. That is their way of praising their Creator. God put the knowledge in them that they can fly. I took flying lessons when I was about 30 years old, so I deeply appreciate what they can do when they are six weeks old.

There are other animals that mature inside the egg. Turtles, snakes, and even dinosaurs laid eggs. The egg contains all the nutrients and codes of DNA and building materials for the egg to mature into the animal of which it is.

Perhaps someone will soon explain why the

chicken crossed the road.

not, neither do they reap, nor gather into barns; yet your heavenly Father feedeth them. Are ye not much better than they?"
Matthew 6:26

"Can that which is unsavoury be eaten without salt? or is there any taste in the white of an egg?"
Job 6:6

Notes:

51

The Work of Hot Coals of Fire

When it comes to grilling hamburgers I am really a purist, in that I like to use natural charcoal. I purchased a gas grill some time ago for the sake of convenience, but for genuine lip smacking flavor natural charcoal is the best. I start by building a small pyramid of charcoal and then with a little lighter fluid start my fire. The chunks of charcoal take a while for the fire to spread over them, then die down, and the coals become live with red inside and a grey ash on the outside. It takes a while, but is worth the wait.

Once all the coals are ready I will spread them out and get ready to do some serious cooking. I let the cooking grate get hot, and then I can cook the best hamburgers. Lightly grilled on the outside and very juicy on the inside.

The cooking process brings the food up to temperature and then kills harmful bacteria, making the food fit for consumption. The cooking process purifies the food.

Hot coals were used when Isaiah the prophet stood before the LORD in Isaiah 6:5-7,

"Then said I, Woe is me! for I am undone; because I am a man of unclean lips, and I dwell in the midst of a people of unclean lips: for mine eyes have seen the King, the LORD of hosts. Then flew one of the

seraphims unto me, having a live coal in his
hand, which he had taken with the tongs
from off the altar: And he laid it upon my
mouth, and said, Lo, this hath touched thy
lips; and thine iniquity is taken away, and
thy sin purged."

Isaiah had seen the LORD of Hosts, the LORD God, and realized that he was just a sinful man. Then he acknowledged the fact he was sinful, and then the angel took the live coal from the altar to touch Isaiah's lips to remove his sin. So the coals are an example of making pure once again.

Another thing live coals can do is help resolve anger issues. In short, if someone has wronged you or not been kind to you, you should still be kind to them. The kindness which you show is very powerful in that person and can help resolve the issues. In Psalm 140:9-10,

"As for the head of those that compass me
about, let the mischief of their own lips
cover them. Let burning coals fall upon
them: let them be cast into the fire; into
deep pits, that they rise not up again."

With some folks it might take a while, and with others it will happen quickly, but it works. That is why Jesus told us to turn the other cheek.

ADDITIONAL SCRIPTURES:

"If thine enemy be hungry, give him bread to eat; and if he be thirsty, give him water to drink: For thou shalt heap coals of fire upon his head, and the LORD shall reward thee."
Proverbs 25:21-22

"Therefore if thine enemy hunger, feed him; if he thirst, give him drink: for in so doing thou shalt heap coals of fire on his head. Be not overcome of evil, but overcome evil with good."
Romans 12:20-21

"Ye have heard that it hath been said, Thou shalt love thy neighbour, and hate thine enemy. But I say unto you, Love your enemies, bless them that curse you, do good to them that hate you, and pray for them which despitefully use you, and persecute you;"
Matthew 5:43-44

"That ye may be the children of your Father which is in heaven: for he maketh his sun to rise on the evil and on the good, and sendeth rain on the just and on the unjust."
Matthew 5:45

"The north wind driveth away rain: so doth an angry countenance a backbiting tongue."
Proverbs 25:23

"And he answered, Thou shalt not smite them: wouldest thou smite those whom thou hast taken captive with thy sword and with thy bow? set bread and water before them, that they may eat and drink, and go to their master."
II Kings 6:22

Notes:

52

The Power of a Blessing

When I embarked into the ministry some years ago I wanted to do something special for those folks attending each service. Traditional services are just that, sort of *cast in stone* for how things are to be done. I gave this a lot of thought, knowing that my choices would be limited.

In my Bible reading time I once again read in Numbers chapter six the famous blessing that God told Moses to tell Aaron and the priest to do.

"And the LORD spake unto Moses, saying, Speak unto Aaron and unto his sons, saying, On this wise ye shall bless the children of Israel, saying unto them, The LORD bless thee, and keep thee: The LORD make his face shine upon thee, and be gracious unto thee: The LORD lift up his countenance upon thee, and give thee peace. And they shall put my name upon the children of Israel, and I will bless them."
Numbers 6:22-27

As pastor, I desire the best for all people of the church. I know that some will have a week ahead of work, some have school, some have to travel, and others have medical issues to deal with. In short, when the people leave through the doors of the church they embark once again on life. The devil is out there just waiting for an opportunity to pounce. It would be impossible for me to be with all of them and help, but I know someone who is ever-present at all times that can be with them, and that is the LORD God.

So began this journey into the power of the blessing. At the end of each service, before we dismiss, I will give the people a blessing from the scriptures. It is my opportunity to put the LORD's name upon them.

I have discovered that the Bible is full of blessings, all intended to teach us God's love for us and His desire for our lives. Now that I am searching for a new blessing, I will find them throughout scripture. I get excited because for now I have found another blessing in scripture to give to the people. I hope you will look for them too.

The power of the blessing is that *we are committing our future to God and that He will make our way right.*

Parents and Grandparents have the power of giving a blessing to their children and grandchildren as they start their day.

"Be strong and of a good courage, fear not, nor be afraid of them: for the LORD thy God, he it is that doth go with thee; he will not fail thee, nor forsake thee."
Deuteronomy 31:6

Remember that children are a heritage of the LORD. The children need to know we are asking God to keep them and protect them. Encouraging words are powerful that God will direct their day and give them courage on their spelling or math test at school.

A pastor can bless his congregation; a Sunday school teacher can bless the individuals in the class.

In closing, I would like to share a few blessings from scripture:

"Blessed is the man that trusteth in the LORD, and whose hope the LORD is."
Jeremiah 17:7

"And the LORD shall guide thee continually, and satisfy thy soul in drought, and make fat thy bones: and thou shalt be like a watered garden, and like a spring of water, whose waters fail not."
Isaiah 58:11

"Thou wilt keep him in perfect peace, whose mind is stayed on thee: because he trusteth in thee. Trust ye in the LORD forever: for in the LORD JEHOVAH is everlasting strength:"
Isaiah 26:3-4

One final thought, I believe there is a blessing in *passing on a blessing* to someone else. It is OK to say "Have a good day". However, don't forget to say "May the

LORD God bless you." As I close I say "May the LORD God bless you."

ADDITIONAL SCRIPTURES:

"O taste and see that the LORD is good: blessed is the man that trusteth in him."

Psalm 34:8

"O LORD of hosts, blessed is the man that trusteth in thee."

Psalm 84:12

"And therefore will the LORD wait, that he may be gracious unto you, and therefore will he be exalted, that he may have mercy upon you: for the LORD is a God of judgment: blessed are all they that wait for him."

Isaiah 30:18

"He that handleth a matter wisely shall find good: and whoso trusteth in the LORD, happy is he."

Proverbs 16:20

"Blessed is the man that walketh not in the

counsel of the ungodly, nor standeth in the way of sinners, nor sitteth in the seat of the scornful. But his delight is in the law of the LORD; and in his law doth he meditate day and night."

Psalm 1:1-2

"Blessed are the poor in spirit: for theirs is the kingdom of heaven. Blessed are they that mourn: for they shall be comforted. Blessed are the meek: for they shall inherit the earth. Blessed are they which do hunger and thirst after righteousness: for they shall be filled. Blessed are the merciful: for they shall obtain mercy. Blessed are the pure in heart: for they shall see God. Blessed are the peacemakers: for they shall be called the children of God."

Matthew 5:3-9

Notes:

ABOUT THE AUTHOR

Bro. Louis has had requests for this second book, "On the Road to Roxton Texas." He is pleased to offer this book, only desiring that it will be a source of encouragement and blessing.

Louis A. Holmes was born in 1954 in a hot and dry West Texas town where his dad worked in the oil fields. His formative years were spent as a preacher's kid in the small North Texas town of Grapevine. Presently, he is the bi-vocational pastor of First Baptist Church in Roxton Texas. Raised in a preacher's home, he has many life experiences to draw from, all with an application to God's Word.

Jan, his wife of nearly 42 years, is an important part of his ministry. They have three children, Eric, Erin, and Michelle. Louis and Jan also have two grandchildren, Jovie and Zed.

The Church in Roxton asked Bro. Louis, as he likes to be called, to write and publish encouraging articles in the Roxton newspaper, *The Roxton Progress.* God has truly blessed the effort, and Bro. Louis is praying that the articles are making a difference in the lives of his readers.

The details of both books can be reviewed and purchases made at www.maxholtmedia.com or directly from www.amazon.com.

www.ingramcontent.com/pod-product-compliance
Lightning Source LLC
Chambersburg PA
CBHW060233050426
42448CB00009B/1419